# HOW ART HEALS

## EXPLORING YOUR DEEP FEELINGS USING COLLAGE

Andra F. Stanton | Foreword by Tien Chiu

SCHIFFER PUBLISHING

4880 Lower Valley Road · Atglen, PA 19310

OTHER SCHIFFER BOOKS BY THE AUTHOR:

*Dimensional Cloth: Sculpture by Contemporary Textile Artists*, ISBN 978-0-7643-5536-3

OTHER SCHIFFER BOOKS ON RELATED SUBJECTS:

*The Art for Joy's Sake Journal: Watercolor Discovery and Releasing Your Creative Spirit*, Kristy Rice, ISBN 978-0-7643-5767-1

*The Art of Weaving a Life: A Framework to Expand and Strengthen Your Personal Vision*, Susan Barrett Merrill, ISBN 978-0-7643-5264-5

*Intersection: Art & Life*, Kevin Wallace, ISBN 978-0-7643-5519-6

Designed by Ashley Millhouse
Cover design by Jack Chappell
Type set in Adorn Roman/Abril Text

ISBN: 978-0-7643-6146-3
Printed in India

Specific art supplies are mentioned in this book. They may be covered by various copyrights, trademarks, and logotypes. Their use herein is to serve as suggestions only. The author does not endorse any specific product, and she has made every effort to use the correct spelling and capitalization of trademarked products. All rights to these products are reserved by their respective owners.

Published by Schiffer Publishing, Ltd.
4880 Lower Valley Road
Atglen, PA 19310
Phone: (610) 593-1777; Fax: (610) 593-2002
E-mail: Info@schifferbooks.com
Web: www.schifferbooks.com

For our complete selection of fine books on this and related subjects, please visit our website at www.schifferbooks.com. You may also write for a free catalog.

Schiffer Publishing's titles are available at special discounts for bulk purchases for sales promotions or premiums. Special editions, including personalized covers, corporate imprints, and excerpts, can be created in large quantities for special needs. For more information, contact the publisher.

We are always looking for people to write books on new and related subjects. If you have an idea for a book, please contact us at proposals@schifferbooks.com.

To all who have
experienced joy and
known sadness

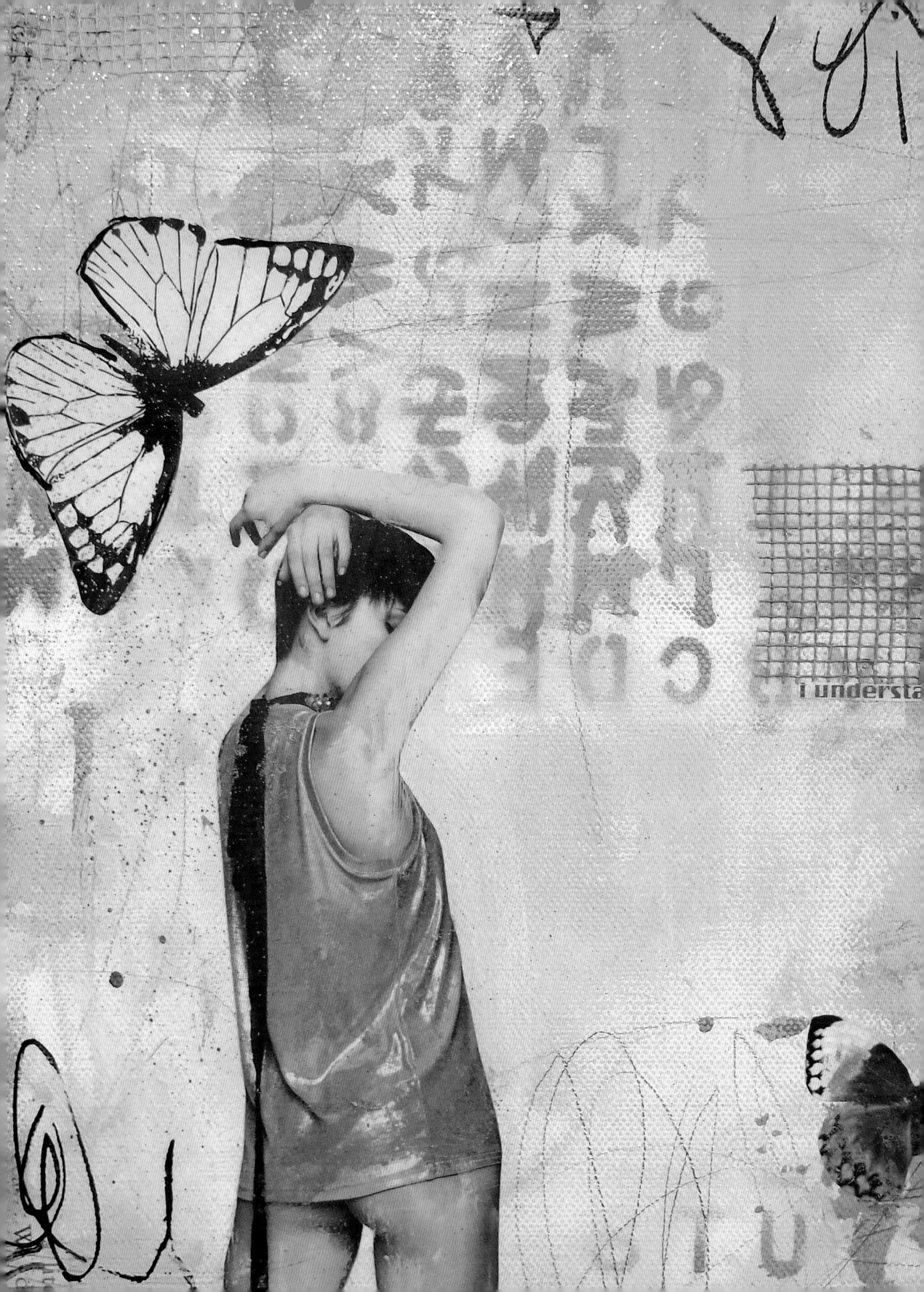
I understa

# Contents

Foreword . . . . . . . . . . . . . . . . . . . . . . . . . 6

Preface . . . . . . . . . . . . . . . . . . . . . . . . . . 8

Acknowledgments . . . . . . . . . . . . . . . . . . 11

Introduction . . . . . . . . . . . . . . . . . . . . . . . 12

CHAPTER 1:
Collage . . . . . . . . . . . . . . . . . . . . . . . . . . 25

CHAPTER 2:
Collage Gallery . . . . . . . . . . . . . . . . . . . . 35

CHAPTER 3:
Exploring Imagery . . . . . . . . . . . . . . . . . . 46

CHAPTER 4:
Getting in Touch with Your
Deeper Feelings . . . . . . . . . . . . . . . . . . . . 55

CHAPTER 5:
The Art Makers and
Their Healing Art . . . . . . . . . . . . . . . . . . . 62

Additional Artists . . . . . . . . . . . . . . . . . . 204

An Invitation to All . . . . . . . . . . . . . . . . . 206

Bibliography . . . . . . . . . . . . . . . . . . . . . . 207

Resources . . . . . . . . . . . . . . . . . . . . . . . . 208

# Foreword

## Art heals.

In 2003, the regenerative power of art saved my life. I had been battling severe bipolar depression for almost a year. Every day, I wrestled with horrible visions, obsessed over every mistake I'd ever made, and fought off suicidal compulsions. Every day, I hand-spun 50 or 60 yards of yarn on a drop spindle (one of the most ancient human tools) and knitted a few more rows on my "Spiral of Life" shawl, which contained motifs representing everything I held dear in life. I designed the shawl as I went, so each row—like a continuing life—was different from the one before and from the one after.

The spinning and knitting kept my hands busy, the rhythmic handwork soothed my troubled mind, and the symbolism transmuted my pain into prayer. My curiosity and the suspense engendered by the "story" of the work helped keep me alive. I wanted to see how the shawl would come out, how the story would end.

By the time the shawl was done, my doctors and I had found a medication that ended the bipolar depression. My "Spiral of Life" shawl helped me stave off the worst of the pain and end the downward spiral of suicidal thinking. It helped save my life.

Although not everyone's life has been saved by art, almost everyone has been touched by art in one way or another. Art helps us connect to and express our deepest emotions. Working with our hands satisfies a deep, human craving to make. And sharing our art with others, if we choose to do so, lets us share our feelings with the world.

In *How Art Heals: Exploring Your Deep Feelings Using Collage*, Andra Stanton offers a way to reconnect with your artistic self by using the accessible medium of collage. Collage is simple enough for a beginner but can also challenge the experienced artist. Andra offers a gallery of collage for inspiration, but whether your work looks like anything in the galleries is irrelevant. As the author emphasizes, your art is for you. You need not worry about whether your art looks better or worse than anyone else's. It only needs to please you.

Andra also offers guided imagery exercises designed to help you connect to and express deep emotions through your artwork. These kinds of exercises are valuable both for finding and processing particularly meaningful or intense memories, especially painful ones, and for finding artistic inspiration. Often, these are one and the same.

The last portion of the book, the gallery of artwork, is particularly invaluable. Ever since the first artist picked up a stick to draw in the dirt, art has been used for telling stories, and stories have been used to connect, transform, and heal. The gallery of art, in a wide variety of media, shows the many ways artists have transformed pain and grief into beauty—through the meditative work of their hands.

If you have suffered emotional trauma or have deep feelings struggling to find expression, *How Art Heals* will help you connect to your creativity. It will inspire you, free you, and offer you practical help and guidance as you find your way to the healing power of art. May you find joy and peace there.

### Tien Chiu

—Former board president, San Jose Museum of Quilts and Textiles
Sunnyvale, California

# Preface

As a former psychotherapist of twenty-five years, I've heard many stories of suffering. As an individual living with multiple medical problems—including curvature of the spine (scoliosis), first discovered in my teens, and chronic fatigue, since the 1990s—and having grown up with a mentally ill parent, I know about suffering personally. I'm sure you, too, know of suffering, whether it is your own or of a relative, partner, or friend.

Suffering accompanies loss—and who hasn't experienced loss? Loss presents us with a painful break in a meaningful relationship with a person, pet, home, or community. The temporary or permanent loss of one's good health can result in a complicated reckoning with mortality itself. Big or small, loss takes an emotional toll.

Naturally, we would all like to turn away from suffering—from sadness, anger, and grief. It's not fun. Most people do, in fact, turn away from it, denying that something sad or painful happened, or is happening, in their lives. American culture certainly encourages us to do so. We're supposed to be happy all the time.

But this can be a huge mistake. The only real way to get past grief is to go through it: to feel it, cry about it, talk about it.

And, possibly, to express it through art.

I have always found comfort in pursuing art and crafts. As a child, I drew with pencil and paper and used a cheap box of watercolor paints, the kind you could get from convenience stores that carried a little of everything, like Woolworth's, *way* before Michael's and JoAnn's.

I couldn't have said so back then, but spending time using my imagination through drawing and painting probably enabled me to feel in control while growing up in a scary dysfunctional family. In retrospect, I see that it gave me both solace and joy.

As an adult, I'd abandoned art and crafts until after my third surgery to improve my spinal curvatures, when I was in my fifties. I was forced to take months off from my job to recuperate, affording me unexpected free time. At first, I got into making traditional quilts, but I eventually found the process more tedious than satisfying, because sticking to the patterns—and having to render them so they fit together perfectly—seemed arduous and limiting. Rather, I wanted to use fabrics like paint to make abstract art, the way oil and acrylic painters use their materials.

When the world of art quilting began to flourish, and I caught wind of it, I finally found like-minded creatives who incorporated new ways of approaching the use of color and shape. I learned from their books and workshops how to construct intuitive, freestyle designs. At the same time, I took up collage, at first using only paper, then paper and fabric—marrying my two preferred media—and composed inventive, often narrative tableaux. At some point during the past five years, I discovered three-dimensional fabric sculpture and became smitten with that art form as well. (I wrote a book about it in 2018 called *Dimensional Cloth: Sculpture by Contemporary Textile Artists.*)

These days, when I stitch the surfaces of my pieces, the patterns emanate from my history, colored by the lack of a nurturing home life and, later, the loss of my health. Each object I create represents moments of meditation on the psychological safety of solitude, but also the joy of connection to friends and to nature. My need to compose—to sit quietly with my feelings as I find a way to bring objects of visual satisfaction to fruition—fuels my curiosity and determination while allowing me to gently explore past or current grief. My art is an attempt to balance distortion and beauty and is a testament to the endurance of the human spirit.

I wrote *How Art Heals* because I know there are those of you who want to explore your own deep feelings, whether from a loss you've encountered in your life or in the life of a loved one, or from the happiness and joy that is also part of life.

Representing your experiences in artistic form is a way of working through trauma or celebrating good luck. When you express and share what you are going through, or what you've been through, it helps the loneliness of suffering fade and can augment a happy event.

Sharing your feelings through your art creates a sense of community, an understanding among participants that—for all our differences—we are, at last, human. With the support and loving kindness of others who also know the pain of loss, and the treasure of good cheer, we can reap the pleasure and medicinal capacity of affinity and connection.

As you read this book, you will encounter the stories of artists and nonartists who used art to communicate their emotions. When they finished their projects, they noticed their sorrow was transformed. They no longer felt the need to hang on to it. All could let it go, at the very least temporarily, but often permanently.

Among these makers, you'll meet Kazuki Takizawa, who creates blown-glass sculptures that resemble goblets that, metaphorically, contain his emotions related to his experience with depression and thoughts of suicide. Wen Redmond manipulates digital photos and prints them onto textured and colored fabric. Her series depicting nests helped her understand her feelings about her children growing up and leaving their own nest. Grace Gee altered an eyeglass case to resemble a coffin, symbolizing her reaction to the demise of her marriage.

For everyone, in one way or another, making art not only afforded relief, but also a boost in self-confidence—and hope. It can do the same for you.

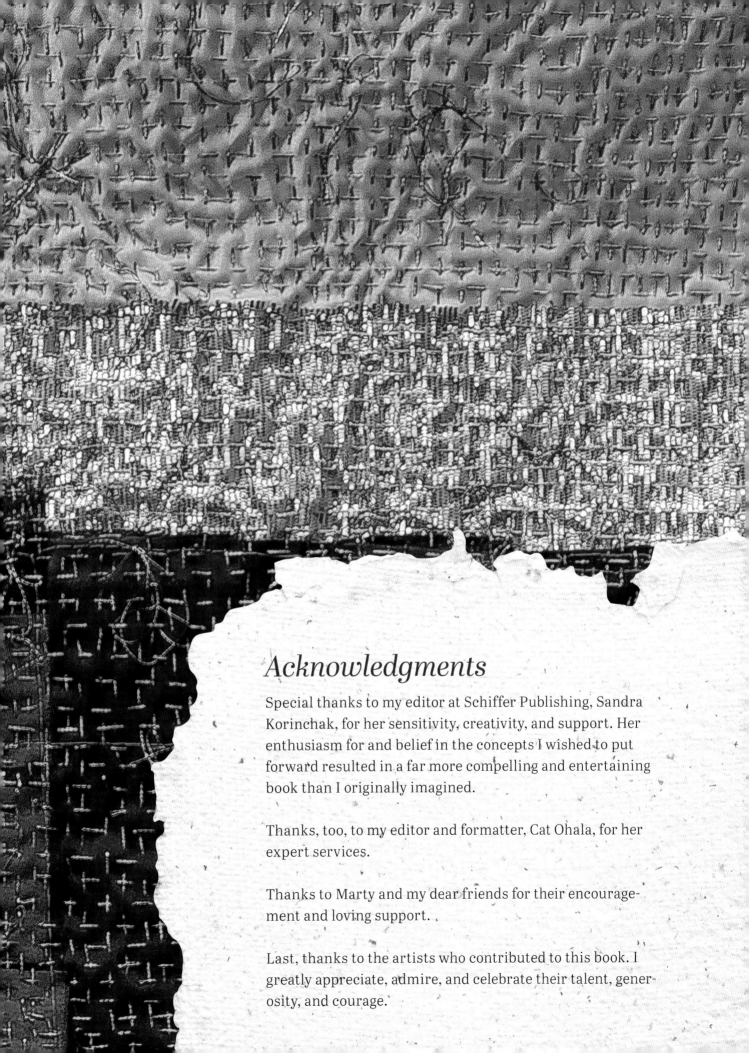

## Acknowledgments

Special thanks to my editor at Schiffer Publishing, Sandra Korinchak, for her sensitivity, creativity, and support. Her enthusiasm for and belief in the concepts I wished to put forward resulted in a far more compelling and entertaining book than I originally imagined.

Thanks, too, to my editor and formatter, Cat Ohala, for her expert services.

Thanks to Marty and my dear friends for their encouragement and loving support.

Last, thanks to the artists who contributed to this book. I greatly appreciate, admire, and celebrate their talent, generosity, and courage.

# Introduction

## The History of Art

From the time our prehistoric ancestors began moving out of Africa, about 60,000 years ago, or even before, *Homo sapiens*—that's us—made art. It's entirely possible that Neanderthals, an earlier version of us, made art as well.

In 2018, researchers found a cave in the thick jungles of Borneo, Indonesia, that holds what is now considered by some to be the oldest figurative cave art ever produced. It dates back approximately 40,000 years and is a depiction of a wild ungulate (hoofed animal) as well as stencils of human hands.

It turns out that such drawings—of animals and hands—have been found throughout the world, with the exception of Antarctica. Astonishingly, they are nearly identical to one another wherever they have surfaced. Did our early ancestors fall in love with making art and teach subsequent generations—over millennia—how, where, and what to draw? Was it a family affair or community-sponsored art academy? A kind of clearinghouse that distributed instructions and materials?

For reference, think of the better known cave art at Lascaux, in France, produced about 17,000 years ago. There, you can see nearly six hundred images of animals, including herds of horses, sharp-horned bulls, and ibex adorned with ornate antlers. They were rendered in red, black, and yellow pigments derived from a complicated processing of grinding, mixing, and heating natural minerals, such as hematite (red) or manganese oxide (black). Some source material was apparently found locally and some acquired from far-flung locations. Painting techniques used included finger-drawing, applying pigment with "brushes" made of hair or moss, and blowing the pigment over a stencil (a human hand) onto the wall with a hollow bone.

Why go through all the trouble? What were the cave drawings used for? Why was it so important to our forebears to create them?

We can speculate, but we'll never really know the answers to these questions.

One thing is sure, however: humans like to make art. It comes naturally to us. By the age of two or three years, most children will pick up a marking instrument, perhaps a crayon or pencil or stick of chalk, and scribble. At first, these marks consist of disorganized broken lines, with no correlation to visual images—evidence that a child's interest seems to result primarily from the handling of the materials and the pure joy of physically making marks.

However, with repetition and concentration, and as their motor control improves and their mind grasps the concept of drawing as a means to explore and communicate about their visual world, the scribbles become representational. At first, young children draw figures floating in space, unrelated to anything. By seven or eight years of age, most begin to see the relationship between things in the environment and themselves. This awareness is indicated by the use of a baseline—a line that demarcates the ground or floor. Now the figures become more realistic. They aren't objects in space, but people standing on earth—no longer abstractions. Next, a story can be invented about those people. By adolescence, children have transitioned from an uninhibited period of thinking and creating and move on to the critical awareness of adulthood—and here is where many of us get stuck.

Self-conscious and self-doubting, we stop making art. We put aside and, more often than not, forget the pleasure derived from experimenting with line, shape, color, and story. Like a muscle that does not get used, our motivation and ability to make art atrophies. We begin to tell ourselves we don't need or want art as a central or even peripheral activity in our lives; other pursuits take precedence.

This is what happened to me until I was forced to retire in my fifties. I was then given the opportunity to reinvent myself. I'd never identified myself as an artist—and I still have a hard time doing so, even though most of my work has been accepted and shown in gallery exhibitions across the country. I don't support myself selling my artwork; therefore, in my mind, I am not worthy of considering myself an artist. I know I'm not the only one who demeans her artistic interests in this way. I have a great deal of company in that regard.

Why should it be this way? If everyone starts out as an artist, as a person making art, why do we need to prove—to ourselves and to everyone else—we are artists? Why do we devise criteria to meet and impose these high standards on ourselves and our work before we feel we can own our creativity? And, most important, what do we lose when we do so?

It turns out we lose a very important tool in our well-being toolbox.

Although the therapeutic effects of the arts have been surmised for decades, it is only in recent years that systematic and controlled studies of these effects have proved this notion to be true. In 2016, for example, researchers determined that making and viewing art decreases a stress hormone in our bodies called *cortisol*. And making and viewing art increases a chemical in our brains responsible for pleasure: *dopamine*.

## *Art Reduces Stress*

Researchers Kaimal, Ray, and Muniz investigated the impact of visual art making on the cortisol levels of thirty-nine healthy adults. Participants provided saliva samples to assess cortisol levels before and after forty-five minutes of art making. At the end of the session, participants also provided written responses about the experience.

The researchers concluded that making art resulted in statistically significant lowering of cortisol levels. Participants' written responses indicated they found the art-making session to be relaxing, enjoyable, and helpful for learning about new aspects of themselves.

*Source*: Kaimal, Giriia, Kendra Ray, and Juan Muniz. "Reduction of Cortisol Levels and Participants' Responses following Art Making." *Art Therapy: Journal of the American Art Therapy Association* 33, no. 2 (2016): 74–80.

So, art can reduce our stress and give us pleasure. What's more, art calms the autonomic nervous system and, in doing so, restores hormonal balance and stimulates brain neurotransmitters, so that both the maker and the viewer of art may access more readily an inner world of imagery and emotion. Such a feeling state can lead both to self-compassion and compassion toward others.

## Art Improves Our Immune System

In another experiment, two hundred young adults detailed how much they experienced wonder and amazement in a given day. Researchers then obtained samples of gum and cheek tissue and found that those who claimed to have experienced greater levels of wonder and amazement had the lowest levels of cytokine interleukin 6—a marker of inflammation.

Researchers linked the awe we feel when touched by art, nature, and spirituality with lower levels of inflammatory cytokines, which are proteins in the body that signal the immune system to work harder. In other words, when we are filled with awe, inflammation goes down, leading to the healing of areas previously damaged by inflammation.

*Source*: Stellar, Jennifer E., Neha John-Henderson, Craig L. Anderson, Amie M. Gordon, Galen D. McNeil, and Dacher Keltner. "Positive Affect and Markers of Inflammation: Discrete Positive Emotions Predict Lower Levels of Inflammatory Cytokines." *Emotion* 15, no. 2 (2015): 129-33.

Studies tell us, then, that art heals by altering our physiology and mental attitude. The body's physiology changes from one of anxiety to one of deep relaxation—from helplessness and fatigue to creativity and inspiration. Art creates hope and positive feelings as well as helps us cope with difficulties. It has the capacity to transform our entire outlook and way of being in the world.

## *Art Soothes Negative Emotions*

Researchers analyzed more than one hundred studies about the impact of art on health and the ability to heal. The studies explored five visual arts: painting, drawing, photography, pottery, and textiles. Each of these studies examined thirty patients who were battling chronic illness and cancer. The findings included the following

- Art reduced depression, stress, anxiety, and negative emotions.
- Art improved well-being and positive identity.
- Art allowed the expression of grief.
- Art led to improved participation in social networks.

*Source:* Stuckey, Heather L., and Jeremy Nobel. "The Connection between Art, Healing, and Public Health: A Review of Current Literature." *American Journal of Public Health* 100, no. 2 (2010): 254-63.

## Art as a Diary

Although we may never know why our prehistoric ancestors painted outlines of animals in caves, it seems clear that today's creators make art for a specific reason. In modern times, art is autobiography. It is the story of "I."

Even if people simply copy a nature scene before them—say, a river bending through thick marsh—the resulting painting tells us as much about who created it as the landscape depicted. Creating art is tantamount to saying, "I am here. This is what I see. This is what I think. This is how I feel."

Art makers show us the world as they experience it. If artists are skillful and can imbue their artwork with their feelings, the work comes alive, transformed by their emotional response rather than simply representing an impressionistic or technical rendering. Think of van Gogh's magical trees and sky—how the implied movement, through swirls and quick brushstrokes, captures and conveys the artist's joy and wonder.

# Art Can Reflect Our Troubled Times

Being alive can be wonderfully exciting, but it can also cause much grief, particularly in troubled times, such as those in which we're living. Every day we're bombarded with headlines in the news that speak of hatred, violence, greed, and corruption among politicians and others who hold power, and those citizens who identify with them. Not just here in America, but all across the globe.

The world feels more dangerous than it has for a long time, with greater than ever levels of hunger, poverty, and uncertainty in our daily lives. We're worrying about toxic greenhouse gases, the wholesale extinction of species of plants and animals, the death of our oceans and the life they sustain, melting polar ice, and the rape of rainforests. We worry about our children going off to school and never coming home because of adults with access to ever-more-deadly weapons. We worry about children of color playing in the streets and being singled out by inadequately or poorly trained police. We worry about our health and the health of those we love, and whether we'll be able to afford and have access to safe and effective medical care. We worry about not being able to pay our bills, of losing our homes, of living on the streets. These are stressful, often cruel times. I'm talking about America—my home—one of the most so-called advanced cultures in the world.

Besides addressing this wretchedness head on, we need outlets. We need ways to take a break from our worries, even if just for a little while. We need bits of time to heal from the onslaught of troubles that exist around us or within us. We need dopamine—our natural pleasure chemical—to help us cope. We need art.

# Art Leads to Compassion

Suffering is part of the human condition, yet society pressures us to feel good—or, rather, act like we feel good—and be "positive." One of America's worst crimes, according to cultural historian and social critic Morris Berman (2000), is the cultivation of a "culture of hustling." Hustling, he says, is the sacrifice of life to consumer culture. It is energizing and often enriching, but ultimately empty, depressing, and destructive. Berman's writings, including *The Twilight of American Culture* (Berman 2000) and *Why America Failed*, take the view that our culture is in a free fall and our citizens are divorced from their true selves.

In an interview in 2013, published in the digital edition of *The Atlantic* magazine (Masciotra 2013), Berman stated:

> *Most Americans have a dull sense that their lives are fundamentally "off"—because for the most part, they are. They hate their lives, but to get through the day, besides taking Prozac and consulting their cell phone every two minutes, they talk themselves into believing that they want to be doing what they are doing. This is probably the major source of illness in our culture, whether physical or mental. . . . To dull your sadness with cell phones or food or alcohol or TV or laptops is to suppress symptoms, and not live in reality. Reality is not always pleasant, but it does have one overriding advantage: It's real.*

One solution, Berman suggests, is to learn to bear the unbearable: to acknowledge and be cognizant of our pain (Masciotra 2013). Here is where art comes in. It serves as an invitation to sit with our sorrow, to be present with our bereaved souls. Bereavement is often approached in our society as a problem that needs a cure, but loss and grief are inherent in living. They do not need to be "treated." The process is essentially a spiritual one, requiring contemplation and turning inward to confront our sadness.

When we give in to our grief, over time we learn to understand and accept it better. We can recognize the path we took from experiencing it when it was most acute, then traveling to when it became something more familiar and less destructive.

With these experiences, when we look into the eyes of someone else who has known suffering, we know what they know, and there is something reassuring in the mutual recognition. Hence, acknowledging our own grief leads to empathy: compassion for others. Grief has the potential to bring us closer to the warmth and connection that is between us.

Yet, society discourages grief—even scorns it—beyond a brief period. Modern culture has adopted an edict around loss, grief, and death. According to this edict, sadness, anger, and sorrow all are dark emotions, the products of an immature mind. The edict is based on the presumption that happiness is the only true measure of health. However, acceptance by others and companionship as we suffer are the only real medicines for grief.

Grief can come from many different kinds of loss, such as divorce, moving, job loss, illness, or death. People who are grieving may express anger, sadness, emptiness, loneliness, and hopelessness. Feelings may come all at once or in a wave of raw emotion or may manifest as fatigue, exhaustion, pain, or the inability to sleep. All of this is normal. We should stop shaming ourselves and others for going through this process. For if we are not willing to feel our grief, if we run from it, sometimes turning to substance abuse, gambling, consumerism, promiscuity, recklessness, or social withdrawal, our lives only get worse.

## Art Becalms Difficult Feelings

Through art, the expression of the inexpressible allows us to reach deep into our heart and mind and peek at the mystery of who we are, what makes us tick. Healing through art is based on the belief that our mental images can help us understand ourselves and therefore enhance our life through self-expression.

It turns out that our deepest feelings and thoughts have a language of their own—a language that uses imagery rather than words. These images aren't always easy to translate into words, but they are an expression of our most authentic and honest responses to our daily lives. Imagery is preverbal—pictures that come to mind before we have time to put a name to them, to assign them meaning through spoken language.

The human brain is a complex organ. It weighs about 3 pounds and contains about a hundred billion neurons, with a hundred trillion connections between them. Divided into two halves, or hemispheres, each half houses regions that control certain brain and body functions. The two sides work dependently, always in coordination with each other, but there's a big difference in how they process information.

Research into the human brain suggests that the left and right hemispheres differ in their handling of abstraction. The left handles abstract thinking and is comfortable designing tools with which to master and understand the world. It is thought to be the more detached (unemotional), rational, acquisitive, conceptual, literal, verbal, and analytical part of our brain. In contrast, the right hemisphere is engaged, empathetic, receptive, intuitive, and holistic. It is involved more with new experiences, new events, ideas, words, and skills while they are still fresh in the mind.

In short, the right hemisphere lets us experience our lives; the left dissects it. To put it another way, the right side of the brain takes in all of our experiences and their corresponding emotions as images, and then the left side of the brain translates those images into verbal thoughts.

The concept of right-brain and left-brain thinking originally developed from research conducted during the late 1960s by Roger W. Sperry, an American psychobiologist, who was awarded a Nobel Prize in 1981 for his research. According to Sperry's theory (Lienhard 2017), people with a dominant right brain are more creative. However, scientists have since found *there is no right- or left-brain dominance*, and this theory has since been labeled as one of the great myths of the brain. The truth is, being creative involves both sides of the brain. We need both logical, abstract thought and intuitive, engaged, empathetic thought to come up with a project and find a way to execute it.

It stands to reason, if our most authentic thoughts and feelings are first formed in the mind as images, then imagery—rather than words—is the most direct way to get in touch with whatever is bothering us, and then these images can be rendered into art.

When we don't know how to express frustration and anger safely, whether through imagery or words, we often waste a lot of energy holding down the upwelling of these feelings. We might succeed for a time, but the frustration and anger eventually leak out or explode all at once, sometimes with destructive results: we turn people away and jeopardize our personal or professional relationships, or we make rash decisions and mistakes, because our energy is caught up in our anger. As soon as we learn to make our unhappy emotions known, not only can we release those feelings, but we can also reap the rewards of being honest with ourselves by acquiring a better understanding of our motivations.

If you're like many people, you might not even realize when you're hurt or angry. After all, most of us have been taught to squelch our so-called negative emotions and be "happy." But your body sends out signals, such as tense muscles, restlessness, or moodiness, to alert you to the fact that something is awry.

One way to connect with, and ultimately release, your feelings is to bypass your verbal thoughts. It's not enough to give your feelings a label: pain, angry, hurt. You have to "see" them as images. Anger may take the shape of a closed fist, for example, or a smoking volcano. More typically, however, our thoughts and feelings are made up of less obvious imagery. For example, when I got in touch, through hypnotherapy, with my desire to access my imagination, it was represented by a polished stone given to me by another version of myself.

Being able to bypass verbal language to find the original images behind language is known as being imagistic. Some people are naturally better at it than others. No matter. Shifting your awareness away from thoughts and toward your mind's images takes practice. Although some people see an actual image, others get only vague impressions. There are others still who aim for but don't see images at all. Often, though, when they approach their art materials after relaxing their mind, they know what they want to compose.

The easiest way to access your own pictures is by using a relaxation procedure called *guided imagery.* Gentle but powerful, guided imagery focuses the imagination, bringing on a naturally immersive altered state. It is fundamentally a form of self-hypnosis used to access, observe, and manipulate images that surface when you are relaxed and nonjudgmental.

With your newly discovered imagery, you can begin to make art that is particular to you, personal art that takes your mindful constructions and makes them visible, to be observed and perhaps studied for insight into the thoughts and feelings driving your behavior. You might find that your inner world has surprises for you. A rose may not just be a beautiful flower, but an object you associate subconsciously with a particular person, place, or event. Accessing this wisdom promises to give you not only a better understanding of what makes you tick and a deeper connection to your authentic self, but also individualistic, meaningful art.

In this book I provide guided imagery exercises as well as instructions for how to collage what you see and feel. Keep in mind that the act of making art out of a happy emotion extends your happiness; art created from stressful emotions releases chemicals in your body that make you feel better.

## Art Helps Us Grieve

Art allows a time and place for contemplation, self-reflection, and story-telling. It allows us to become aware of and to value the uniqueness of our perceptions and abilities. It might be the most direct way of learning about ourselves—not only our authentic emotions, but also how we approach challenges and failures during the process of creation. An openness to these experiences counteracts mindless conformity and leads to a sense of self-empowerment. Art makers gain appreciation, through their artwork, of the value of their singular contribution to their life and to the world.

Art has the potential to address every possible problem and offer its transformative power to those in need of comfort. For those who use art to describe their emotional and physical suffering, art is a process during which they may come to a full understanding—and, perhaps, acceptance—of the tragic event in their lives.

The process of grieving is an internal one, a searching within of thoughts and feelings of sadness, anger, emptiness, despair, loneliness, and hopelessness. These are the ways in which the body and mind deal with the shock of loss. Grief, then, is an attempt to restore equilibrium and recreate meaning in our shattered lives. Grief's goal is to find a new way to carry on.

People who are grieving need friends and loved ones to be with them as they move through it. This is crucial, because the course is such that, once past the acute period, grief emerges and falls back, moving from the foreground to the background many times over.

We must serve as witnesses to others' pain, without judging and without pushing for premature resolution. If we encourage grieving people to "get over it," "put it behind you," or "stop talking about it" or instruct them about the so-called power of positive thinking, we end up making them feel even more alone and misunderstood than they already feel, and we may feel helpless and then resentful.

The more we practice staying with our own grief or the grief of others, the more we trust our ability to experience grief fully. The more we experience it—*feel* it—the more comfortable we are at allowing it to happen, rather than suppressing and denying it, which is a losing battle. Our ability to look at rather than turn away from personal tragedy leads us, ultimately, to develop acceptance of our genuine feelings.

## Art Heals

While writing this book, I interviewed one hundred artists. You'll see the work of fifty of them here. If you want to see the work of the other artists, please go to **www.schifferbooks.com/HowArtHeals**.

### *Work by Other Artists*

If you want to read about more artists—other than those presented in this book—and see their work, head over to **www.schifferbooks.com/HowArtHeals.**

Each artist was asked to submit artwork that was an expression of either deep grief or great joy. For those in pain, after describing the source of their grief, they then explain how they felt when they completed their artwork. To mark this change, their transformative experience is written in italics. Nearly all stated that the process of making their art caused a significant shift in their lives.

For many, it was as if they took their grief and imbued their art with it and, in doing so, transferred the pain from inside to an object outside themselves so that it no longer resided within them. The art became like a talisman, a charm, to hold their grief. At last, they were again in control of their lives. Grief was no longer controlling them.

These artists are sculptors, art quilters, glassmakers, metalsmiths, painters, weavers, digital artists, and more. Most share hardships they were forced to confront, and they did so through the process of making art, examining their broken hearts with a sense of respect and reverence. This focus gave them space to be exactly as they are, without needing to clean up their emotional mess or rush through it. They approached their sorrow with compassion and care.

Anxiety over confronting an unwanted outcome often discourages many from making art, and this is unfortunate, especially because those who could use art to express either their happiness or pain don't give themselves this potentially life-changing opportunity. To make art is to open the door to possibility, to be moved profoundly, and perhaps to move others as well.

*We all learn to live with disappointment and sadness. Not everything works out in the end. We need a way to acknowledge, experience, and perhaps communicate our pain. Creating art can help, if we can find the courage to pursue it despite its own challenges.*

# CHAPTER 1

# Collage

Henri Matisse (1869-1954). © *Jazz*, 1947. Portfolio of twenty pochoirs.
Composition: various; sheet: 16.75″ × 25 ¹¹⁄₁₆″
Publisher: Tériade Éditeur, Paris; Printer: Edmond Vairel and Draeger Frères, Paris. Edition 250. The
Museum of Modern Art, Gift of the artist, 1948. © Succession H. Matisse / Artists Rights Society (ARS), New
York. Digital Image © The Museum of Modern Art / Licensed by SCALA/Art Resource, NY

With art, every age for millennia has left its unique imprint on the world. From those first cave paintings to the ceiling of the Sistine Chapel, to Byzantine sacred and secular illuminated manuscripts, to the graffiti paintings of Keith Haring, art tells the story of our evolving notions of who and what we are.

Surrealist artists, part of a cultural movement that began during the early 1920s characterized by artwork that featured unexpected juxtapositions, made extensive use of collage. They invented the subgenre Cubomania collage, for example. This artwork was made by cutting an image into squares that were then reassembled at random.

Contemporary collage art has grown beyond cut-and-paste to encompass assemblage and mixed-media approaches. Furthermore, artists are using this process to address urgent social and political issues as well as painful personal experiences.

## Are You Ready?

If you can tear a piece of paper and glue or tape it down onto another piece of paper, you can make art. You might get lucky and actually like your first artistic creation, or it might take time and practice to make art that satisfies you. This is true for everybody, even famous artists.

The point is, you have to start at the beginning and work your way up. Or not. There really is no need to aspire to anything more than you can do now. This art is for you and you only. It's your little secret, unless you decide to share it with someone else. And you might decide you don't want to—for any number of reasons, and all your reasons are legitimate. Be respectful of your right to your own privacy.

Collage allows your creativity to run wild. It lets you combine media to create something entirely novel. Borrowed (that is, copyright-free) and/or hand-produced images can be combined, and they can be set against colored and patterned backgrounds. The "world" you create will be unique to you.

If you ask practiced artists how they approach composing their art projects, all undoubtedly have their own set of steps. Some fabric artists I know, for example, who begin with a gorgeous piece of fabric but have no idea what to do with it, told me that the first step is to cut it up and rearrange it, look at it from different angles, and perhaps throw in some other fabrics to see how they all "play" together.

These pieces tend to start as abstract art—that is, art that's not supposed to look like anything. They aren't a specific object, scene, or landscape, but simply a celebration of shape, color, and composition. As the artist moves the pieces around and introduces new elements, however, they might become an impression of a specific object, scene, or landscape. And if a photograph, say, is placed upon it, it might become a background for a literal image. All of this is achieved simply by cutting up materials.

Some artists spend time sketching out their ideas on paper, in sketchbooks, or in art journals before approaching their collage substrate. All or most of the final piece is worked out before they begin to assemble it. Others start by cutting out a meaningful shape—a symbol important to them—and then build a composition around it. Still others know only the feeling they want to express, and start from there.

In other words, everyone is different. You won't know your own preferred strategy until you start making your own art.

I recommend first making art about things that fill you with happiness. Perceiving and expressing beauty or wonder brings about a sense of renewal, wonder, passion, and life-affirming energy. My favorite subject for years was my cat!

At this point you might be thinking, *I can't draw!* Not to worry. You can take images from photos, newspapers, magazines, and the internet. You can use any of those images as long as you don't intend to sell your art. If you do intend to sell or exhibit it, make sure your images are not copyrighted or that they are sufficiently cut up so the original image has become unrecognizable. The laws on copyright continue to be ambiguous. It's better to be safe than sued.

## Basic Materials

The following is a list of all the basic materials you need to collage. If you don't have them around the house, try local and online art and craft stores, and thrift shops. See the "Resources" section at the end of this book too.

1. **A substrate, something sturdy to which you can attach your images, such as**
    - a piece of cardboard (such as from a cereal box)
    - a painting panel
    - stretched canvas
    - a piece of flat wood
    - Bristol board
    - watercolor paper
    - mat board
    - foam core board
2. **Sharp scissors or a rotary cutter and cutting mat**
3. **Glue, such as**
    - PVA glue

- archival glue (such as Lineco Neutral pH)
- permanent glue stick (such as UHU)
- gel medium or matte medium (such as Golden or Liquitex)
- YES Stickfast Adhesive
- Mod Podge

4. **Paper, for tearing and cutting (Remember, if you plan to exhibit or sell your work, images must be your own, not copyrighted. There are royalty-free image websites.)**
   - marked-up printer paper (with pens, pencils, paint markers, etc.)
   - magazines
   - catalogs
   - newspapers
   - royalty-free digital images
   - book pages
   - junk mail
   - scrapbook paper
   - postcards
   - maps
   - playing cards
   - greeting cards
   - wrapping paper
   - origami paper
   - metallic paper (such as from yogurt containers)
   - wax paper
   - candy or food wrappers
   - decorative paper
   - wallpaper

5. **Marking instruments (optional)**
   - graphite pencils
   - colored pencils
   - markers (black, white, colored)
   - paint pens
   - crayons
   - watercolor paints and brushes (such as Koi)
   - acrylic paints and brushes (such as Liquitex Basic)
   - spray acrylics (such as Jaquard)
   - spray inks (such as Dylusions)
   - white or black gesso (makes paper less porous so you'll use less paint; creates a white or black background or lightens bright colors or patterns)

## 6. Embellishments (optional)
- fabric strips and pieces
- rubber stamps and ink pads
- stencils
- buttons
- postage stamps
- feathers
- needle and thread or sewing machine to make stitches
- dried leaves, twigs, or flowers
- small, flat metal washers
- beads
- pieces of lace
- decorative tape (such as Washi tape)
- modeling paste (such as Golden or Liquitex)

## 7. Copyright-free digital imagery
- stocksnap.io
- burst.shopify.com
- dreamstime.com (requires sign-up, but it's free)
- unsplash.com
- pixabay.com
- gratisography.com
- pexels.com
- allthefreestock.com
- freerangestock.com (requires sign-up, but it's free)
- freestocks.org
- pictography.com
- gettyimages.com (go to Embed Viewer)
- bigphoto.com
- campfight.com
- skitterphoto.com
- publicdomainpictures.com (requires sign-up, but it's free)
- lifeofpix.com
- libreshot.com
- cupcake.com
- stockvault.com
- littlevisuals.com
- mischiefcircus.com

8. **Workplace organization**
   - drop cloth, old towel or old sheet, newspaper, or plastic sheeting to cover and protect your work surface
   - paper towels
   - baby wipes
   - cardboard or plastic containers to hold and store your tools and materials
9. **Preservative (if you want your work to survive for years)**
   - Golden Isolation Coat
   - UVLS acrylic polymer varnish (such as Golden)
   - soft, synthetic wide brush

# Getting Started

## Have an Idea

The easiest way to start is to find a topic or theme that interests you. I suggest you choose a fun and pleasurable one for your first collages.

Here are some ideas:
- a pet
- a friend
- home
- a sport or hobby
- an artist whose work you admire
- a peaceful scene
- peace in the world
- black and white
- one color
- squares, rectangles, or circles
- a garden
- flower bouquet
- numbers
- alphabet
- hands
- birds
- a dreamscape
- chairs
- music
- windows
- doors
- maps
- earth
- sky
- mountains
- water
- germination

## Make a Background

Cover your work surface with a drop cloth, newspapers, or a piece of plastic and place your substrate on top. You may want to cover both sides of paper substrates with acrylic medium to strengthen them. You may also want to cover the front of canvases with medium to make it less absorbent, especially if you plan to use paint. In both cases, wait until the medium dries completely before proceeding.

Start laying out a background by using torn light-colored or neutral paper (such as newspapers or pages from an old book). Glue them to your substrate. After you have covered some, most, or all of your substrate, let your adhesive dry.

Take a look at your substrate. If the papers you used are too dark or the patterns or marks too pronounced, this is a good time to apply, unevenly, diluted white paint or white gesso with a crumpled-up paper towel over the entire spread. If you've used too much and can't see your background papers anymore, rub some off with a wet paper towel or baby wipe. Allow the substrate to dry.

Now you can begin to illustrate your idea or theme with your colored papers, photos, drawings, and/or embellishments. Save for last the strongest image that represents your theme; this will become your focal (main) image. Find an arrangement that pleases you, and then glue everything down. There is no wrong or right way to do this; it all depends on what looks good to you.

After you have adhered everything to your substrate, you might want to add some colors and/or marks. Easy marks include circles, x's, and a column of short, straight lines. These tend to pop out if made in black or white or any other color that is in contrast to what you have so far.

## Choose a Focal Point

Take your strongest image—the one that represents your theme—and place it just off center, slightly up or slightly down on the substrate. I'll tell you why you might consider doing this in the next section. After you have adhered your focal image, go ahead and add whatever embellishments look relevant to your theme or just look fun.

If you want to preserve your work for the long term (years), so that it doesn't dry out, collect dust, or fade from the sun (especially if you used acrylic paint), apply with a clean, soft brush a coat or two of undiluted gloss medium or Golden's Isolation Coat followed by an application (with another clean, soft brush) of diluted (one part water to three parts varnish) polymer varnish, using long, gentle strokes.

Varnishes are available in three finishes: matte (no shine), satin (slightly shiny), and gloss (very shiny and reflective). The one you choose depends on the look you're after. You might need to try them all out on a scrap collage to see how they look. The matte finish, for example, might lighten dark collage papers and paint.

# Composition Basics

You might be interested in knowing where to place elements of a design so the overall composition delivers impact and balance. The following sections describe some tried-and-true compositional placements.

## The Rule of Thirds

*The Rule of Thirds* draws viewers in and compels them to look at your art long enough to see what you have done and what you have to say.

To understand how to use the Rule of Thirds, picture a box evenly divided into three vertical columns and three horizontal columns, creating nine parts. Now imagine positioning your strongest image at the intersection where any two lines meet.

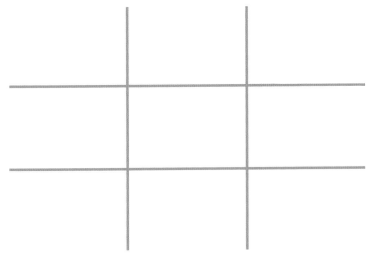

Understanding the Rule of Thirds

### The Center Rule

According to *the Center Rule*, the main subject should be off-center because the eye is naturally inclined to settle on a point to the right and slightly above the center. The rule really should be called *the Not Center Rule.*

### The Allover Rule

*The Allover Rule* says all the visual elements in your composition need to work together, without any element taking over the picture. A focal point should be surrounded by interesting imagery and/or marks that enhance it, rather than obscuring or overpowering it. Think of the background elements as orchestral music and the focal image being a soloist's contribution to the symphony.

### Other Simple Design Rules

*Landscape*, in our context, is a term that describes the format—not the content—of the collage. In other words, you can use it to illustrate any subject, not just a scene in nature. Essentially, according to landscape design, elements are shaped into bands of varying width and placed in horizontal rows, one above the other (horizontal landscape) or next to each other (vertical landscape). One to three larger, simply colored, and patterned bands lead observers to look more carefully at the visually active (patterned, marked, illustrated) narrow strips. You can see a nice example of a horizontal landscape format in the Collage Gallery in chapter 2. Look for Bambi Lyn's *Sea of Souls*.

*Cruciform* is another design strategy. It refers to a cross shape. The areas that form the arms of the cross are generally busy, whereas the four corner quadrants are relatively quiet or even empty. In practice, this format is harder to identify when analyzing artwork because it is not as obvious as, say, a landscape design. But if you keep a basic cross shape in mind as you construct your collage, this can be a helpful way to organize your elements. Look for Pascaline Marange's collage *Untitled* in the Collage Gallery in chapter 2.

Congratulations! You've just made a collage!

As you view the collages in the next chapter, keep in mind that you don't have to follow any rules. You can make up your own rules! Your collages are for *you*. They are meant to be a courageous and pleasurable way to tap in to and visualize your thoughts and feelings.

# Collage Gallery

The collages in this chapter were created by artists and nonartists. They used basic techniques similar to those I described in chapter 1, and digital collage as well. Digital collage requires advanced knowledge of Photoshop or similar image-editing programs. According to this technique, you choose online images and manipulate them, adding layers and "texture" (actually, images of texture). You can print the finished collage and add more layers with markers, paint, and ephemera—or not.

Janice McDonald. *Opening*. 10″ × 10″ × 2″. http://www.janicemcdonald.com. Photo courtesy of the artist.

Pascaline Marange. *Untitled*. 9″ × 13″. www.collage-du-dimanche.com. Photo courtesy of the artist.

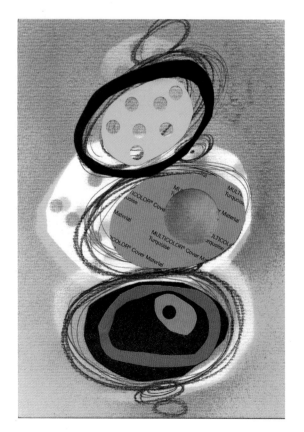

Rebecca Collins. *Cellular Abstract*. 5″ × 7″. http://rebeccacollins.com. Photo courtesy of the artist.

Lorette C. Luzajic. *I Understand Your Loneliness*. 12″ × 12″. www.mixedupmedia.ca. Photo courtesy of the artist.

Bambi Lyn. *Sea of Souls*. 8" × 10". www.etsy/mymedievalmind. Photo courtesy of the artist.

Elizabeth St. Hilaire. *Wekiva Meander*. 10" × 20". www.paperpaintings.com. Photo courtesy of the artist.

Elaine Langerman.
*Passion*. 10″ × 13″.
www.elainelangerman
art.com. Photo
courtesy of the artist.

Denise Cerro. *Black Birds on a Wire*. 7″ × 5″.
www.denisecerrostudio.com. Photo courtesy of
Nate Castner.

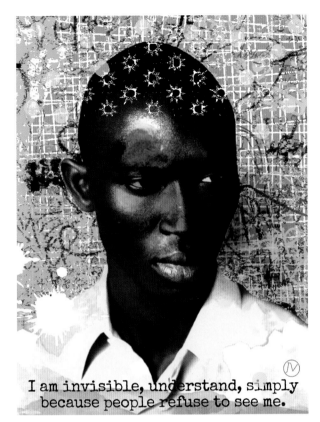

James Vath. *Invisible Man*. 9″ × 12″. www.facebook.com/Meta-Collage-407973226708676/. Photo courtesy of the artist.

Denise Cerro. *Life Still Standing*. 20″ × 16″ × 1.5″. www.denisecerrostudio.com. Photo courtesy of the artist.

Nancy Goodman Lawrence. *Insight and Vision*. 8″ × 8″. www.nancygoodmanlawrence.com. Photo courtesy of the artist.

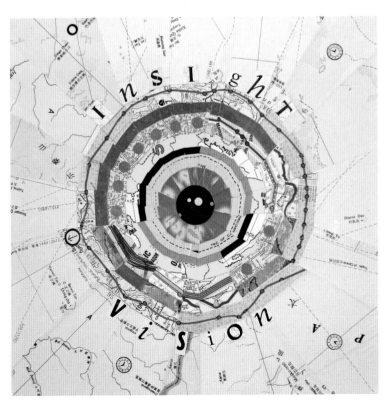

Susan Brown. *Play Date*. 24″ × 36″. https://susiebrownart.com. Photo courtesy of the artist.

Mary Marley. *Evacuate*. 30″ × 22″. www.maryamendolamarley.com. Photo by Graham W. Marley.

Denise Cerro. *Lost Days*. 14″ × 10″ × 1″. www.denisecerrostudio.com. Photo courtesy of Nate Castner.

Cindie Gittelman. *Tatiana*. 11″ × 14″. https://collagepainter.com/. Photo courtesy of the artist.

Susanne Belcher. *Revelation*. 14″ × 11″. www.susannebelcherart.com. Photo courtesy of the artist.

Elizabeth St. Hilaire. *Western Bluebird #2*. 10″ × 10″. www.paperpaintings.com. Photo courtesy of the artist.

James Vath. *Blue Coyote (American Gods)*. 8″ × 12″. https://facebook.com?Meta-Collage-407973226708676/. Photo courtesy of the artist.

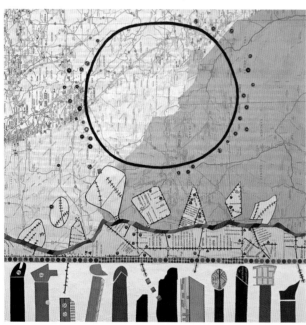

Nancy Goodman Lawrence. *Place #6*. 16″ × 16″. www.nancygoodmanlawrence.com. Photo courtesy of the artist.

Kathy Leader. *Then the Skies Will Soon Be Blue*. 15″ × 20″. www.kathyleaderstudio.com. Photo courtesy of the artist.

Kathy Leader. *Sediment*. 18″ × 24″. www.kathyleaderstudio.com/. Photo courtesy of the artist.

Nancy Goodman Lawrence. *Ori.* 23.5″ × 31.25″. www.nancy goodmanlawrence. com. Photo courtesy of the artist.

Janet Black. *Serenity.* 14″ × 14″. http:// janetblackart.com. Photo by Greg Montano.

Trayc Claybrook. *Apple 7*. 12″ ×
12″. www.traycclaybrook.com.
Photo courtesy of the artist.

Lili Francuz. *Vortex*. 36″ × 36″.
http://lilifrancuz.com/. Photo by
Michael Loughlin.

# CHAPTER 3

# Exploring Imagery

Now that you've made a collage, you understand the basics of how it helps you visualize your thoughts and emotions. You're ready to try using art to explore and express more difficult feelings. Art therapy techniques, like guided imagery activities, are a way to tap into these deeper emotions.

## What Is Art Therapy?

According to the American Art Therapy Association, art therapy is defined as the use of art as a form of psychotherapy for people experiencing trauma or illness, seeking personal development, or struggling to deal with day-to-day living. It takes place in a multitude of settings, including medical centers, senior centers, veterans' clinics, K–12 schools, community programs, crisis centers, and private and public mental health offices.

The purpose of creating art in art therapy is to seek and understand the art maker's accompanying narrative—that is, the story generated by the artist in response to the artwork produced.

## Getting Started: Relax!

Whether you choose to access your deeper feelings by yourself or with social supports, the first thing you need to do is *relax*. The following exercise helps you relax before you move on to the guided imagery exercises. There are many such relaxation techniques on the internet or in books. If you do a search and find another that you prefer, use that one instead.

### *Safety First*

First, before approaching this more challenging work, be honest with yourself. Will you be able to soothe yourself—alone or with the help of friends or family—if and when strong feelings come up? Feelings such as sadness, anger, or agitation? Hopelessness? Rage?

If you have any doubt at all, do not make the attempt to look inward by yourself. Seek the help of a professional mental health caregiver such as a clinical social worker, a counselor with a master's degree or PhD, a psychologist whose training is in psychotherapy, or a psychiatrist whose training included psychotherapy. Or, you might want to seek out an art therapist (see the "Resources" section at the end of the book).

## BELLY BREATHING

1. Lie flat in a comfortable position.
2. Put one hand on your belly, just below your belly button, and the other hand on your chest.
3. Take a deep breath in through your nose and let your inflating belly raise your hand. Your chest should not move.
4. Breathe out. Feel the hand on your belly fall as you push all the air out.
5. Repeat three times, then resume normal breathing. Don't rush.

## CHEST BREATHING

1. Still lying flat, put your left hand on your belly and your right hand on your chest.
2. First, as before, inhale into your belly so that your left hand rises. Then continue inhaling into your upper chest so that your chest (right) hand rises and your belly hand falls.
3. Exhale slowly through your mouth, feeling any tension leave your body.
4. Repeat three to five times. Don't rush.

To get in touch with your emotions, you must go inside your mind and tap into the imagery produced by your right brain. The imagistic impressions of feelings, especially difficult ones such as sadness, grief, anger, and helplessness, will reveal the difference between your verbal, left-brain interpretations of your feelings and your truer, more authentic picture-based right-brain representations. By reconciling the two, you will begin to identify the deeper emotions that plague you and discover a path to emotional healing.

# What to Expect

Be prepared to draw what you see after you finish these guided imagery exercises. Have a paper and a box of crayons or a pencil ready so you can draw what you remember or what you felt. If no specific images come to you during guided imagery, it's OK. Try to focus on your feelings and draw something anyway. This information should help you begin to tell a story for your collage work.

If you have trouble coming up with ideas, the following prompts might spark your thoughts and feelings:

- safe place
- protective wall
- treasured possession
- balance
- gratitude
- core belief
- magic
- my journey
- hope
- connection
- warrior
- passion
- going with the flow
- wisdom
- abundance
- spontaneity
- self-portrait
- compassion
- battleground
- love
- freedom
- evolution
- clarity
- mask
- brave heart
- miracle
- sadness
- waiting
- abandonment
- transitions
- memories
- introspection
- revelation
- the color or shape of pain

## It's OK to Stop

Stop either of the guided imagery exercises that follow if you feel uncomfortable emotionally. Perhaps return to them with a supportive friend or family member or consider doing this work with a professional therapist.

If you're not used to meditating or following guided visualization exercises, the process might feel strange. I remember scoffing before I first tried it. But it works. Please take a leap of faith and give the exercises a try.

Be careful not to judge what you draw. That's your critical left brain talking. Because you may have never done this work before, this "evaluating" part of your brain might find fault with something that it is not familiar with and doesn't quite understand. If you sense you're being critical of your work, close your eyes and take one or more slow belly or chest and belly breaths. You should feel your shoulders drop as you release whatever tension you are holding on to. This will reorient you and get you back in touch with your nonjudgmental right brain.

## Guided Imagery Exercise 1

You might want to record this exercise for yourself, have someone record for you, or have someone read it to you. Remember to pause before reading each sentence. Don't rush.

Put aside about sixty minutes. Wear comfortable clothing. Shut your door for privacy, if necessary and if possible. Sit or lie down on a comfortable chair, lounger, sofa, or bed. Close your eyes when you are ready. Keep your arms at your sides and uncross your legs. If you're cold, cover yourself with a throw or blanket.

When you are settled,
Take a big, slow inhale through your nose.
Exhale through your mouth, pushing out as
much air as you can.
When you are done, go back to breathing
normally.
When you're ready, just begin to allow your-
self to relax,
To let all your cares and worries go.
At this moment, nothing else matters.
As you switch off your thoughts
And allow this time for yourself,
You begin to unwind.
Unwind completely.
And as you begin to feel more and more
relaxed,
Let go of any worries or problems
That have been on your mind lately.
They soon drift out of your mind.

Take a deep breath,
Slowly filling your lungs with fresh air.
And as you exhale,
You will relax more and more.
With every exhale,
As you gently slow down your breathing,
You feel more and more relaxed,
More and more comfortable.

As you feel your entire body sinking down,
Notice how relaxed your whole body has become—
From the top of your head
To the tips of your toes.
Your eyelids are very heavy
And may even twitch
As you let go of any tension in your body.

All the muscles in your jaw have become limp
and relaxed,
And you are beginning to drift down deeper
and deeper.
You feel more and more relaxed with every
word you hear.
As this wave of relaxation spreads down your
neck and shoulders
And all the way down your arms to your
fingertips,
You may feel a tingling sensation in your
fingertips.
As your arms grow as heavy as cement,
You become aware of a growing, peaceful
feeling inside.
A feeling of calmness and contentment.
You are doing very well.

As you feel every muscle in your chest and
abdomen become limp and relaxed,
All the muscles in your back relax.
And all the way down your spine,
The muscles loosen and relax.
And as you drift down deeper and deeper,
And feel more and more relaxed,
You let this wave of relaxation spread all the
way down your legs,
So that your legs feel as heavy as cement.
Every muscle in your legs is limp and relaxed.
You are completely relaxed—
From the top of your head
To the tips of your toes.

And as the outside world
Fades more and more into the background,
You begin your journey into your own inner
world,
To that unique and special part of you,
That only you can go to.
You continue to let go.
Any sounds around you fade into the
background.
You are doing very well.

As you continue to go deeper and deeper,
Into a lovely state of relaxation,
You may find that your mind begins to
wander.
And it doesn't matter where you drift,
Where you go.

In a few moments,
You will hear the word
*Now.*
And when you hear the word
*Now,*
Your body
Will continue to sink down,
Becoming more and more limp,
More and more relaxed,
And comfortable.

Feel yourself sinking down,
Becoming even more comfortable,
Feeling completely at peace,
Calm and contented,
As you continue to drift down,
Truly enjoying this wonderful feeling of
complete relaxation.

Soon you will see a welcoming staircase in
front of you,
A staircase going down.

*Now,*
See the staircase.
See the lovely carpeting on the stairs.
Take a moment to admire it.
It is a beautiful staircase.
Look down to the bottom of the staircase.
It has ten steps,
And you want to go down the steps.
They are warm and welcoming.
They are warm and safe.

At the bottom is a golden light,
A glow,
And it pleases you.
And when I tell you to, you will go down these
ten steps,
One at a time,
Feeling more and more relaxed,
Feeling your sense of relaxation deepen and
deepen.
You are doing very well.

When you hear the word
*Now,*
You will take your first step down,
Feeling comfortable and calm,
Feeling relaxed.
Take a moment to feel how deeply relaxed you
are.

*Now,*
Take the second step down the stairs,
Feeling comfortable and relaxed,
And keeping your eyes on the stairs below
you.

*Now,*
Take the third step down, becoming even
more relaxed,
More calm,
More comfortable.
Take a moment to inhale deeply and slowly.
Let the inhale out slowly, slowly,
Before breathing regularly again.

*Now,*
Take the fourth step down,
Feeling unhurried and carefree.
Take a moment to notice how deeply relaxed
and carefree you feel.

*Now,*
Take the fifth step down.
You are halfway down,
And you will continue to go down,
Down into deeper relaxation,
Feeling calm and comfortable.
*Now,*
Take the sixth step down,
Feeling deeply relaxed.
Notice how your feet feel against the step.
Notice how balanced and steady and secure
you feel.

*Now,*
Take the seventh step down,
As you sense how deeply relaxed and con-
tented you feel.

*Now,*
Take the eighth step down.
You are almost to the ground floor.
Notice how relaxed, contented, and comfort-
able you feel.

*Now,*
Take the ninth step down,
As you notice how calm and carefree you are
feeling,
Relaxed and content.

*Now,*
Take the last step down to the ground floor.
You are doing very well.

You are on the ground floor.
In front of you,
You see a welcoming door.
Take a moment to notice the door
And what it looks like,
What it's made of,
Feeling deeply relaxed.

Go to the door and pull the door open.
The scene you see is beautiful.
Before entering the scene,
Inhale slowly and deeply.
Let your breath fill you with comfort and
calm.
Feel your calm as you let your breath out
slowly and completely.

*Now,*
Focus on the scene in front of you.
See how beautiful the scene is.
Take a moment to observe the beautiful scene.
Take a moment to feel how relaxed and calm
you are.

*Now,*
Walk into the scene in front of you.
As you walk, take a moment to feel the per-
fectly warm air around you.
Feel it move ever so gently on your arms and
face.
Notice how you feel perfectly warm, but not
too warm.
As you look around, notice the perfect light
surrounding you.
Notice how the light makes the scene even
more beautiful.
Let yourself wonder at the beauty around you.
Notice how relaxed and open you feel
As you look at the light.
See how it shines on the beautiful scene.

Take a moment to listen to the sounds you are
hearing in this beautiful scene.
Notice how the sounds enhance the beauty of
the scene around you.
Feeling deeply relaxed and calm,
Enjoy the beauty around you.

*Now,*
Inhale slowly and deeply.
Let your breath fill you with calm and peace.
Feel how relaxed you are
As you let your breath out slowly and
completely.

*Now,*
You see a figure coming toward you.
The figure is smiling.
You watch, calm and relaxed, as the figure
greets you.
Perhaps you know this person.
Do you recognize him or her?
Perhaps you don't know who this person is,
But you have a strong, unmistakable sense
That this person feels warmly toward you.
Take a moment to notice how good you feel
seeing this person.

Before the figure turns to leave, he or she
leans toward you
And places something in your hand.
It is something you need.
It is something you've been longing for.
Take a moment to observe it.
Notice how relaxed and comfortable you feel
as you observe it.

Then the person smiles warmly and says
goodbye.
Feeling relaxed and calm,
You also say goodbye.
Take a moment to savor how relaxed and
warm you feel at this moment.

*Now,*
It is time to come back to the place where you
are sitting or lying.
I will count to three
And when you hear *three*,
You will awaken.
When you hear *three*,
You will open your eyes,
Feeling relaxed and peaceful.
When you awaken,
You will feel a desire to communicate what
you experienced.
You will want to express what you felt.
You will want to use art to express what you
saw and felt.
One.
Two.
*Three.*

## Postexercise Questions

1. What did your scene look like?
2. Did you recognize the figure who approached you?
3. How did that person make you feel?
4. What did the figure give you?
5. What does that object mean to you?
6. How did you feel?
7. Can you choose an image or set of images that came to you or
   inspire you to create a picture or collage?

# CHAPTER 4

# Getting in Touch with Your Deeper Feelings

# Guided Imagery Exercise 2

You might want to record this exercise for yourself, have someone record for you, or have someone read it to you. Remember to pause before reading each sentence. Don't rush.

Put aside about sixty minutes to complete this first exercise. Wear comfortable clothing. Shut your door for privacy, if necessary and if possible. Sit or lie down on a comfortable chair, lounger, sofa, or bed. Close your eyes when you are ready. Keep your arms at your sides and uncross your legs. If you're cold, cover yourself with a throw or blanket.

When you are settled,
Take a big, slow inhale through your nose.
Exhale through your mouth, pushing out as much air as you can.
When you are done, go back to breathing normally.
When you're ready, just begin to allow yourself to relax,
To let all your cares and worries go.
At this moment, nothing else matters.
As you switch off your thoughts
And allow this time for yourself,
You begin to unwind.
Unwind completely.

And as you begin to feel more and more relaxed,
Let go of any worries or problems
That have been on your mind lately.
They soon drift out of your mind.
Take another deep breath at your own pace.
Fill your lungs with fresh air.
After you exhale,
You will relax even more.
You are feeling more and more relaxed,
More and more comfortable.

As you feel your entire body sinking down,
Notice how relaxed your whole body has become—
From the top of your head
To the tips of your toes.
Your eyelids are very heavy
And may even twitch
As you let go of any tension in your body.

Notice that all the muscles in your jaw have become relaxed,
As you drift down deeper and deeper.
As this wave of relaxation spreads down your neck and shoulders
And all the way down your arms to your fingertips,
You may feel a tingling sensation in your fingertips.
As your arms grow as heavy as cement,
You become aware of a growing, peaceful feeling inside.
A feeling of calmness and contentment.
You are doing very well.

As you feel every muscle in your chest and abdomen become limp and relaxed,
All the muscles in your back relax.

And all the way down your spine,
The muscles loosen and relax.
And as you drift down deeper and deeper,
And feel more and more relaxed,
You let this wave of relaxation spread all the
way down your legs,
So that your legs feel as heavy as cement.
Every muscle in your legs is limp and relaxed.
You are completely relaxed—
From the top of your head
To the tips of your toes.

And as the outside world fades more and more
into the background,
You begin your journey into your own inner
world,
To that unique and special part of you,
That only you can go to.
You continue to let go.
Any sounds around you fade into the
background.
You are doing very well.

As you continue to go deeper and deeper,
Into a lovely state of relaxation,
You may find that your mind begins to
wander.
And it doesn't matter where you drift,
Where you go.

In a few moments,
You will hear the word
*Now.*
And when you hear the word
*Now,*
Your body will continue to sink down,
More and more relaxed,
And comfortable.

Feel yourself sinking down,
Becoming even more comfortable,
Feeling completely at peace,
Calm and contented,
As you continue to drift down,
Truly enjoying this wonderful feeling of
complete relaxation.

Soon you will see a welcoming staircase in
front of you,
A staircase going down.

*Now,*
See the staircase.
See the lovely carpeting on the stairs.
Take a moment to admire it.
It is a color you've always liked.
It is a beautiful staircase,
Made of wood, solid and strong.
Look down to the bottom of the staircase.
It has ten steps,
And you want to go down the steps.
They are warm and welcoming.
They are warm and safe.
At the bottom is a golden light,
A glow,
And it pleases you.
And when I tell you to, you will go down these
ten steps,
One at a time,
Feeling more and more relaxed,
Feeling your sense of relaxation deepen and
deepen.
You are doing very well.

When you hear the word
*Now,*
You will take your first step down.
Take a moment to feel how deeply relaxed you
are.

*Now,*
Take the second step down the stairs,
Feeling comfortable and relaxed,
And keeping your eyes on the stairs below you.

*Now,*
Take the third step down, becoming even more relaxed,
More calm,
More comfortable.
Take a moment to inhale deeply and slowly.
Let the inhale out slowly, slowly,
Before breathing regularly again.

*Now,*
Take the fourth step down,
Feeling unhurried and carefree.
Notice how deeply relaxed and carefree you feel.

*Now,*
Take the fifth step down.
You are halfway down.

*Now,*
Take the sixth step down,
Feeling deeply relaxed.
Notice how your feet feel against the solid, sturdy step.
Notice how balanced and steady and secure you feel.

*Now,*
Take the seventh step down,
As you sense how deeply relaxed and contented you feel.

*Now,*
Take the eighth step down.
You are almost to the ground floor.
Notice how relaxed, contented, and comfortable you feel.

*Now,*
Take the ninth step down,
As you notice how calm and carefree you are feeling,
Relaxed and content.

*Now,*
Take the last step to the ground floor.
You are doing very well.

You are on the ground floor.
In front of you,
You see a welcoming door.
Go to the door and pull it open.

You see that you are in a movie theater.
It is a lovely room,
With walls and seats in coordinating colors,
Colors that you've always liked.
The seats are upholstered and look comfortable to you.
You find one that is in a location in the room that pleases you
And you sit in it,
Noticing how relaxed you feel,
And how the room is comfortable and pleasing to you.
Take a moment to feel how relaxed and comfortable you are.

Soft cushions are beneath you.
They are perfectly supporting your spine and the back of your neck.
And as you feel how relaxed you are,

Notice, too, how the air in the room is a perfect temperature,
And the smells around you are fresh and pleasing.
There may be others in the theater
Or you may be the only one there.
It doesn't matter.
You are feeling perfectly comfortable, perfectly relaxed.

The lights in the theater begin to dim;
The movie is beginning.
You sink into your comfortable chair,
Feeling content and interested in what the movie will be about.
You see a home
And it seems familiar to you—
The inside or the outside or both.
You notice some details about the building that remind you of another home.

Take a moment to inhale deeply and exhale slowly,
Feeling deeply relaxed.
It occurs to you that the home you are seeing is *your* home,
The home you grew up in.
You look around and notice familiar objects.
These objects bring to your mind some memories of growing up.
Whether these memories are neutral, happy, or sad
Notice how calm you feel,
How relaxed you feel as you see them.

These objects are memories of things or situations that happened in the past.
Whether pleasant or troubling,
Take a moment to remember this thing or situation

That affected you when you were a child.
Try to identify one of the feelings that you felt,
But remember that you are an adult now,
And are comfortable and relaxed in a lovely theater.

And now see a young version of yourself in the remembered situation.
Notice the expression on the face of your younger self.
Notice how you feel toward your younger self.
Take a moment to identify what you are feeling
As you watch your younger self.
Think of what you would tell your younger self if you could
Or what you would do
Or what you would give—
Something that would resonate with and please your younger self.

Notice that the images on the movie screen are fading.
Take a moment to inhale deeply,
Then exhale slowly and thoroughly.
The images on the movie screen are continuing to fade.
At the count of three, the movie will end
And the theater lights will come up.
You will return to the present,
Keeping your feelings of calm, peace, and relaxation.

One.
Two.
Three.
When you are ready,
Open your eyes and return to full wakefulness,
Feeling alert and refreshed.

## Postexercise Questions

1. How did it feel to see a younger version of yourself?
2. What did you say or do or give to the younger version of yourself?
3. Why?
4. How did you feel?
5. How do you think your younger version of yourself felt?
6. Why?
7. Can you choose an image or set of images that came to you or inspire you to create a picture or collage?

# What to Do Next

Hopefully, as you have just experienced, by using pictures rather than words, you got in touch with feelings inside you without the influence of the judgmental part of your brain. Now ask yourself the following two questions. You can write down your answers in a notepad, journal, or anywhere that is convenient. If you prefer, you can tell your answers to a supportive person who will listen and not judge you. Or, you can discuss your answers with a professional caregiver. However you accomplish this, make sure you answer the questions, because they will enable you to process and understand what you've just experienced.

1. What did you feel as you went through the exercise?

2. What did you learn about yourself—about what makes you happy or about what part of you needs loving attention and healing?

Many people find that accessing emotions through guided imagery and creating a collage based on the images, colors, or shapes that come up during the process is all they need to feel peace and let things go. That is, identifying and simply getting the images *out* can feel transformative.

Some don't feel the need to think more about these images; others seek to create new artwork to reflect more deliberately on their new understanding or to come to grips with what it would take to resolve the difficult emotions they encountered. If you want to, you can use the imagery you discovered, then collage it again as if your troubles have been healed.

For example, I once "saw" my hurt feeling as a closed fist. I made a three-dimensional fabric sculpture to represent it. This was a difficult area to explore, because the fist represented my mother's stroke and it stirred up feelings from the past, feelings related to my contentious relationship with her, as well as the sadness I felt, knowing her health had been compromised. In an effort to soothe those feelings, I held the sculptural fist I'd made between my two hands in an act of forgiveness and compassion, but also as an expression of what I had wanted her to do to my own fist. In doing so, I did experience a soothing of my pain.

I had done this with a gesture—holding the fabric fist—but it could have been equally or perhaps more powerful had I made another fabric sculpture depicting my hands around the fist, or by making a sculpture, drawing, or collage based on forgiveness and the resolution of our mother–daughter rift.

Your guided imagery experience should help you figure out what you need to do next. Only you can decide whether you want to pursue that path. It's important that you realize that transformation doesn't mean you now deny your troubled emotion. It means you are looking at it differently. Exploring and, perhaps, letting go of old ways of thinking and feeling allow for room to have a look at new, more soothing, and more empowering ways of thinking and feeling. It provides a vision filled with possibilities, rather than a dead end, where feelings get stuck, build up, and contaminate your soul.

You will find that old and new wounds *can* heal, but only if you examine and understand them. If you bring compassion and kindness to your pain, healing *can* take place. You will find yourself able to move on in your life. You will free yourself of memories and feelings that might be holding you back from achieving emotional comfort.

You may never completely forgive or forget a painful experience, but you now have tools to access your feelings and soothe them, if not resolve them. And it may be that you do resolve them too. Either way, you give yourself a reprieve—a vacation—and a chance to take care of yourself before going forward.

Art may not make you happy and art may not solve all your problems, but art may very well lead to a physical and emotional release that clears your mind and allows you to heal—one artwork at a time.

# CHAPTER 5

# The Art Makers and Their Healing Art

Narrative art is art that tells a story through imagery. The power of a story is in how and what it makes the maker and the viewer feel. These visual stories hold the possibility of stimulating the imagination, eliciting emotions, and pinpointing universal truths.

Historically, visual narratives depended on the era of their creation. Typical narrative art made before the Renaissance, for example, was controlled by wealthy patrons for social and political power and prestige. After the Renaissance, artists tended to compose elaborate, romanticized scenes of ordinary people, meant to uplift and honor them as they engaged in daily activities.

**Modern art was the first attempt at eschewing narrative.** It was neither representational nor metaphorical. Surrealism, abstract expressionism, conceptual art, and installation art became the new avant-garde. Abstract expressionists, for instance, fill their canvases with fields of color and abstract forms supposedly devoid of meaning.

But narrative art has changed. Contemporary narrative art now aims to criticize and to protest, or to tell intimate stories about personal experiences, creating familiar imagery to which most everyone can relate. It also speaks of imaginary worlds or alternate versions of the future. Using complexity and ambiguity, today's artists offer a fresh and challenging interpretation of the visual narrative.

In the following pages, you will meet fifty artists who share their work with you, along with the thoughts that led them to create it and the transformation they achieved on completion. As mentioned earlier, their transformed feelings and ideas are in italics.

## *Work by Other Artists*

If you want to read more artist stories—other than those presented in this book—and see their work, head over to **www.schifferbooks.com/HowArtHeals**.

Beth Markel. *Unfinished Conversations*, 2018. 61" × 59".
Materials: cotton and dupioni silk fabric
Techniques: piecing by the artist, machine quilting by Becky Collis
Photo by David Roberts

# 1. Beth Markel

WWW.BETHMARKEL.COM/BLOG
MINNESOTA, USA

"*Unfinished Conversations* began slowly as a set of about a dozen blocks whose colors reminded me of the clothes my sister had bought for her first 'real' job. And then the piece took on a life of its own. The more I put together blocks, the more memories flooded back to me. It became a grieving process.

"While creating *Unfinished Conversations*, I kept a journal. Some of my journal writing after my sister passed was very dark. I was angry that she was only fifty when she died. I would ask myself, *How do I want to express these feelings in a visual way?* Hence, so many different blocks representing the many paths my thoughts took me down."

*After completing* Unfinished Conversations— *right down to the last stitch—I felt a tremendous sense of contentment. I had suffered the loss of my sister and best friend, my partner in pranks, my matron of honor, keeper of my secrets. When I was doing the piecing, I'd laugh and cry, remembering our time together. But, after the last stitch, I burst out sobbing. It was a letting go, a complete catharsis, and I felt complete satisfaction.*

Helaine Schneider. *Timeline*, 2013. 8″ × 17″ × 8″.
Materials: clay, metal nails
Techniques: sculpting
Photo courtesy of the artist

# 2. Helaine Schneider

WWW.HELAINESCHNEIDER.COM

FLORIDA, USA

"A timeline is defined as 'a graphic representation of the passage of time as a line.' It is believed that we store our memories in a linear manner in an internal memory storage system. The arrangement of the timeline varies and can be from left to right, front to back, or, in my case, as a spiral. Some of my memories are pleasant; some, not so much. This piece is about the removal of my painful memories, which are represented along my timeline by the rusty nails."

*The process of creating* Timeline *helped me identify the origin of my emotional pain. After it was completed, I felt the negative emotions lift and float away.*

*Being happy does not mean we are not also feeling pain or grief. Sorrow and contentment can coexist.*

# 3. Joyce Watkins King
**WWW.JWKINGART.COM**
**NORTH CAROLINA, USA**

Joyce's piece, *Building a Bridge*, was one of the first pieces she created after having been diagnosed with stage III breast cancer.

"I had made a decision just a couple of months earlier to leave my full-time job. Although my job was fulfilling, it was all-consuming and did not leave me enough time to make art. My plan was to consult half time and make art half time.

"Like many well-laid plans, I had to revise them quite a few times during the following two years, because I became very sick from the chemo and tired from the radiation and surgery I had to undergo. I had to slow down every aspect of my life and learn to accept generous help from friends and family.

"All my life I had been very independent, taking care of myself and others. Hardly ever one to get sick, I always kept up a regular exercise routine and a healthy diet. Everyone was shocked that I had been diagnosed with this disease, but I wasn't really, knowing my mother had been treated for breast cancer a few years earlier and that two of her sisters had died from the disease.

"I was determined to devote time each day to creativity, despite my fatigue, even if it was no more than a sketch or notes in my journal—ideas for future projects. Fortunately, my studio is in my backyard.

"In addition to my family, friends, and faith, I believe that my creativity contributed greatly to my healing process. The act of making, especially abstract work, is so engaging that I would forget, at least for a time, that I was in pain and had a life-threatening disease. My studio time provided an escape from the day-to-day routine of treatments and always afforded me something to look forward to.

Joyce Watkins King. *Building a Bridge*, 2012. Diptych: 24″ × 24″ (each).
Materials: cradled boards, encaustic wax, graphite, hosiery, fabric
Techniques: stitching, drawing, painting
Photo courtesy of the artist

"*Building a Bridge* was partially inspired by the pink and orange fabric scraps that an artist friend had given me. He'd picked them up from the side of the road, thinking they might 'speak' to me. He was right. They found their home in this encaustic diptych as the element that bridged a visual gap between the two sides and held the composition together. The fact that it was a bit dirty and tattered and twisted felt just right as I reflected on what was happening with my own body, battered by drugs that were literally killing my cells, both the good and bad."

*When* Building a Bridge *was completed, I had a gut-level feeling that this piece was successful because it expressed how I was feeling at the time. Also, I thought about how delicate fibers—when twisted together—become strong, and when yarn is woven or knitted into cloth, it becomes stronger still. Although yarn can be as delicate as spider silk or as strong as a suspension bridge cable, both become exponentially stronger when they work together with other strands. Textiles can be very malleable, adjusting to fit their purpose, whether it is clothing, a furniture covering, or a piece of art. This duality of fragility and strength was the perfect metaphor for my cancer journey and my hopefulness that a bridge to a cancer-free future would be found.*

"*Casting a Net* uses similar materials to *Building a Bridge.* It was created shortly after my surgery for breast cancer, when I learned that my type of cancer had been misdiagnosed and I would have to endure another year of treatment. It was both bad news and good news: bad because of the additional time in treatment and good because my actual type of cancer would be more treatable if I were to have a recurrence.

"*Casting a Net* was a form of self-encouragement to remain hopeful about my disease while also accepting the idea that the rest of my life was not certain. I came to realize that nearly every person, every human who lives long enough, will face challenges, tragedies, and the fear of the unknown. For me, learning to live with this fear took practice. Just like the fisherman doesn't know whether he will catch fish on any given day, the act of casting his net is one of hopefulness, of making an effort to move forward despite the unknown."

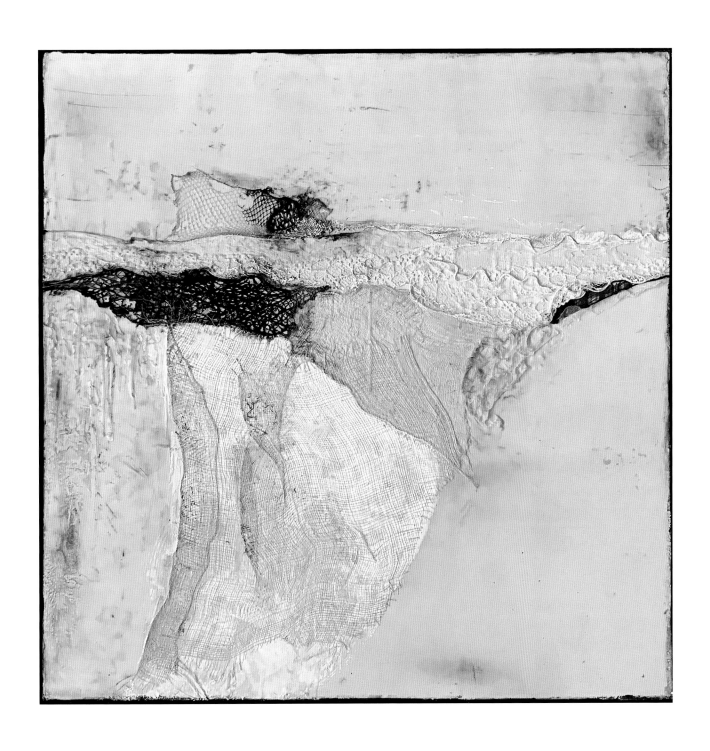

Joyce Watkins King. *Casting a Net*, 2013. 30″ × 30″.
Materials: cradle board, encaustic wax, graphite, lace, netting, hosiery
Techniques: stitching, drawing, painting
Photo courtesy of the artist

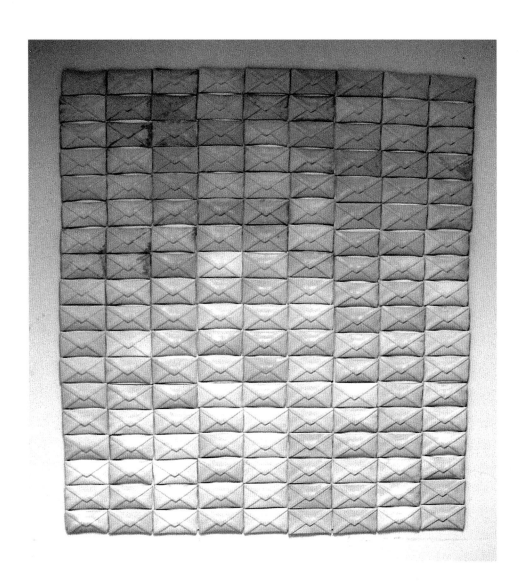

Samantha Stumpf. *Flight or Fight* (162 envelopes representing the number of days of treatment), 2015. 56″ × 52″.
Materials: 162 porcelain envelopes
Techniques: porcelain firing to cone 10, woodworking
Photo courtesy of the artist

# 4. Samantha Stumpf
SLSTUMPF.COM
MARYLAND, USA

"Six years ago, I was diagnosed with non-Hodgkin's lymphoma (mediastinal large B-cell lymphoma). I was unable to work in my ceramic studio while undergoing treatment, which involved six rounds of chemotherapy as well as twenty-one days of radiation.

"While I was home, recovering and attempting to stay connected to the people in my life, and to keep my hands busy, I wrote many letters. It was a moment in time: just me, that person, and the paper. There was no judgment. When I received letters back, it became a moment of connection I needed badly, considering I could not interact physically with many people because of my low white blood cell counts.

"After my treatment was completed and I was able to work in my studio, I created several porcelain envelope projects inspired by the envelopes I'd sent and received. These ceramic installations combine all the moments and stories that I experienced, and ultimately formed quilts of reflection."

*When I completed this piece,* Fight or Flight, *I was very satisfied. It was a conclusion to a milestone in my life. I was able to reflect on the past several months and get back to my life.*

Judy Kirpich. *Anxiety No. 10 / Retirement*, 2015. 43" × 69". Materials: hand-dyed cotton
Techniques: machine-piecing, machine-quilting
Photo by Mark Gulesian

# 5. Judy Kirpich
WWW.JUDYKIRPICH.COM
MARYLAND, USA

Judy has been a graphic designer for the past thirty-seven years. She retired three years ago.

"As much as I was happily anticipating my retirement, I was equally anxious about what it was going to be like to stop going to the office every day, and also what selling my firm would feel like. With *Anxiety No. 10 / Retirement*, I tried to capture my combined emotions of fear and elation."

*I used a process that involves slashing and cutting into cloth over and over. This technique helped me to deal emotionally with my complicated feelings. After finishing the piece, I felt satisfied and actually looked forward to the beginning of my retirement.*

Judy created *Anxiety No. 9 / Mastectomy* after learning of a close friend's cancer diagnosis.

"I started this piece upon learning of her need to have a mastectomy. Because she is of Japanese ancestry, I wanted to incorporate indigo fabric, a fabric traditionally associated with Japan. The large very dark circle symbolizes loss."

*After completing the piece, I still felt sad that my friend was losing a breast. But I felt hopeful that she would be able to beat her cancer—and she did. With this piece, too, I hoped to convey the profound sense of loss that can be experienced not only by the cancer patient, but also by friends and family.*

*Conflict No. 11* is part of a series based on Judy's reactions to the civil war in Syria.

"As ISIL [Islamic State of Iraq and the Levant] moved into Syria, the results were displacement, chaos, and bloodshed. The Syrian population was caught between the repressiveness of the Assad regime, opposition factions, and the terror that ISIL brings. My work tries to capture this ongoing crisis.

"This series uses brutal shapes that are intersecting and bumping into each other. I used a primarily dark palette because I was feeling depressed about the situation. The quilting in this piece is somewhat violent in areas, not orderly. This mirrors my reactions to the conflict."

*Completing this piece did not make me feel relief. Only peace can accomplish that. I just hope the audiences that see this twelve-piece series will be pushed to think more deeply about the Syrian situation and not just skip over articles about it in newspapers.*

Judy Kirpich. *Anxiety No. 9 / Mastectomy*, 2014. 68" × 43".
Materials: hand-dyed cotton, vintage Japanese hand-spun indigo cotton
Techniques: machine-piecing, machine-quilting
Photo by Mark Gulesian

Judy Kirpich. *Conflict No. 11*, 2016. 75.5" × 81".
Materials: hand-dyed cotton, Japanese hand-spun indigo cotton
Techniques: machine-piecing, machine-quilting
Photo by Mark Gulesian

Elizabeth Myers Castonguay. *Ivory-Billed Woodpecker (Endangered body of work)*, 2015. 36" × 48".
Materials: acrylic on canvas
Techniques: painting
Photo courtesy of the artist

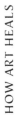

# 6. Elizabeth Myers Castonguay
WWW.CREATIONARTSTUDIO.COM
NEW YORK USA

"*The Ivory-Billed Woodpecker (Endangered body of work)* was painted four years into my working on an Endangered series. This body of work is still ongoing. The paintings generally depict the human form monochromatically, with the more than 40,000 species of endangered wildlife and plant life in full color because they are as important to the fine balance of nature as humanity. I also look for similar visual relationships between wildlife and human form. Because clothing connotes an era or culture, the figures are often undraped to show the universality of the issues that we are facing, such as climate change, deforestation, overfishing, pollution, and poaching."

*My art is created to work on a myriad of levels and to speak in a universal language. I try not to sensationalize or be confrontational, because I want my viewers to internalize, reflect, and see the face of a world that we have painted. Within the work there is urgency, but also an element of hope.*

"*Finished?* uses an undraped, monochromatic figure without a recognizable face to represent a universal victim. Even some global warming doubters began to have second thoughts after Hurricane Katrina, which took the lives of at least 1,833 people, 70,000 pets, and countless wildlife. The storm also cost $81 billion in property damage. The economic repercussions to Louisiana and Mississippi may exceed $150 billion, making it one of the costliest hurricanes in US history.

"It is becoming more and more apparent that it will take global partnerships to control misuse and overuse of natural resources. The United States and the vast majority of the world signed the Paris Agreement in December 2015—a pledge to work together toward a healthier environment. It was a monumental achievement. By November 2016, things began to change in the United States and there was talk of pulling out of the Paris Agreement. Although no agreement is perfect, the Paris Agreement was a beginning step in the right direction. I saw *Finished?* in a dream on election night 2016."

*I knew as a young child that I was going to be an artist and that I had to speak about subjects that I was passionate about. I have always been impassioned about human diversity as well as the Earth and Her creatures. I felt I was blessed with some talent and needed to use that gift to speak. We all have talents and must call upon them to create a more just and healthier world for all species. We were given Paradise but didn't recognize it. We can remedy some of what we have created through global partnership. This is how I view my work.*

Elizabeth Myers Castonguay. *Finished? (Endangered body of work)*, 2017.
30" × 40".
Materials: acrylic on canvas
Techniques: painting
Photo courtesy of the artist

Crista Ann Ames. *Four Years with a Silver Tongued Devil*, 2013. 29″ × 54″ × 32″.
Materials: stoneware
Techniques: coil-building ceramics
Photo by Karl Schwiesow

# 7. Crista Ann Ames
WWW.CRISTAANNAMES.NET
MONTANA, USA

"*Four Years with a Silver Tongued Devil* was extremely difficult to make. It was the first piece in which I tapped into experiences that I was ambivalent about keeping private. I was living with a verbally abusive, alcoholic partner, and I began to believe that something was wrong with *me* because his family and friends didn't believe me when I asked for help.

"While working on *Four Years with a Silver Tongued Devil*, I thought about gestures and postures that I associated with incidents of verbal abuse to help me return to the experience. I also thought of anthropomorphism and how to represent a person who is both wild and tame, docile and dangerous."

*After completing this piece, I felt relief. I discovered the extent to which making art about a difficult experience took the experience outside me and interrupted its ability to control me. Once externalized, an isolating experience became an opportunity for connection and community.*

"The piece *Encircling While Wandering* emerged from an experience during which I was betrayed by a partner and chose to stay in the relationship. The sculpture explored my conflicted impulses to run from pain and to stay attached to a person I loved. I was dealing with questions of fidelity and forgiveness—understanding that those who sometimes hurt us are doing the best they can.

Crista Ann Ames. *Encircled While Wandering*, 2015. 63″ × 36″ × 46″.
Materials: stoneware and fence posts
Techniques: coil-building ceramics
Photo by Karl Schwiesow

"I used *Encircling While Wandering* as a way to externalize and release the mounting anxiety and pain that I was feeling. It enabled me to focus on empathizing with my partner's feelings as I explored my own and communicated them."

*After making this piece, I felt a sense of relief. I also felt a new closeness with my partner. It allowed me to understand him better, to be more confident in my decision to stay with him, and it helped me develop a new level of empathy for other people who have chosen to stay in difficult relationships or have chosen to respond to betrayal and pain with forgiveness.*

· · · · · · · · · · · · · · · · · · · · · · · · · · · · · · · · ·

*Creating gives you a chance to slow down and explore issues in your life. It can be a deeply satisfying way to process and express complex feelings and find relief.*

Anna Kozłowska-Łuc. *Woman and Creature*, 2017. 10" tall.
Materials: ceramic, glazes
Techniques: electric-firing
Photo courtesy of the artist

# 8. Anna Kozłowska-Łuc

WWW.ANNKLUC@GMAIL.COM
WARSAW, POLAND

English is a second language for this artist.

"The source of my inspiration for *Woman and Creature* was a moment in my life when I was waiting for change, when a close friend of the family was going through a terrible illness and I was hoping she would recover. I prayed to God that He would help me bear my sorrow and that He would bring about a good outcome, even though it seemed impossible.

"As I worked on this piece, I felt a little like an observer—that the sculpture was coming to be, almost by itself. This is the best time for me, when my work is in progress."

*The process of creating gives me relief. I always feel this way, except when something goes wrong, when I can't finish what I started to do. But the next day, I can try again. Creating is a time of relief.*

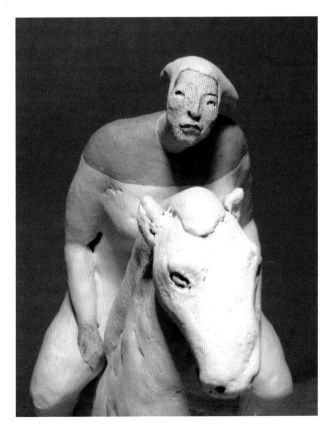

Laurel Siwicki. *The Keeper*, 2017.
19" × 7" × 7".
Materials: ceramic, wire, underglaze
Techniques: sculpting
Photo courtesy of the artist

# 9. Laurel Siwicki

WWW.LAURELSIWICKI.COM
FLORIDA, USA

"Right now my children are young and very close to me, and they depend on me, but I know their growth and development will lead to their independence. I anticipate that I'll be thrilled, but will also miss, when they are grown up, the sweet relationships we have now.

"*The Keeper* holds the bird close to her heart, and there is a very thin string literally tying them together, keeping them connected. She knows she will want to see the bird flourish, and she'll have to let the string go. Her dress is a sort of cage to represent her conflicted feelings. She wants to keep the bird close, but she also wants it to fly away and make a life for itself."

*My works represent specific stories, but I feel the emotions behind them are something we all share. For* The Keeper, *the idea of knowing you want to keep something close to you, but you must let go for it to grow, is something I feel many people can relate to.*

Laurel Siwicki. *Do Not Disturb*, 2018. 17″ × 9.5″ × 9″.
Materials: ceramic, found objects, underglaze
Techniques: sculpting
Photo courtesy of the artist

"*Do Not Disturb* concerns all the things that can stop or interrupt my thoughts along the way as I work on a piece. They can include either outside or internal influences, or both, all of which have the potential to hinder or derail my ideas, which are represented by the nest on the figure's head. The figure is trying to quiet the questions and doubts that might throw her off course."

*While creating this piece, I wondered why this image felt important to me. My mind created it before I understood the emotions behind it. I kept asking myself, What does the figure want to silence and why? I realized this sculpture illustrates the idea that it's important to allow myself to take an idea and follow it to its conclusion, and not second-guess myself because of insecurities or outside opinions.*

Cathy Franzi, *Banksia
anatona*, 2018.
21″ × 8″ × 8″.
Materials: porcelain
Techniques: wheel-
throwing and altering,
sgraffitoing
Photo by Andrew
Sikorski, Art Atelier
Photography

# 10. Cathy Franzi

WWW.CATHYFRANZI.COM

CANBERRA, AUSTRALIA

"My work is based on Australian plants and the environment and comes from my deep love and respect for the natural world. But my motivations are also driven by the pain I feel when environments are destroyed and the biodiversity of species declines, and by my overall concern about climate change. My work is a response to dealing with my love of nature and the grief I feel at its decline.

"I have developed an approach to carving a clay surface based on linoblock printmaking, reflecting the period during the early twentieth century when Australian flora thrived in the decorative arts and print media. The work I make captures the untidy beauty of Australian flora, referencing botanical illustration and printmaking, and alludes to the vulnerability of our diminishing natural environment.

"The critically endangered *Banksia anatona* only grows in Stirling Range National Park in Western Australia. I visited a remote site where it grows to collect seed with staff from the Threatened Species Seed Centre. It was an extraordinary place and experience. It inspired my work here, *Banksia anatona*."

*I feel satisfaction from making and completing. I hope to share my appreciation and love of nature with an audience and draw attention to the beauty and wonder around us. It might be lost as a result of our actions.*

Wen Redmond. *Leaping Point*, 2011. 51" × 32".
Materials: cotton canvas, paint, stabilizer, perle
cotton, UV medium
Techniques: photographic printing onto painted
cotton canvas, using an Epson 2400 inkjet printer,
mounting onto stabilizer, stitching with perle
cotton, sealing edges and top with UV medium
and paint
Photo courtesy of the artist

Wen Redmond. *Pause,* 2011. 25" x 32" x 5".
Materials: photo printed on fabric, molding paste
Techniques: photographic printing onto painted
cotton canvas, using an Epson 2400 inkjet printer,
mounting onto stabilizer, stitching with perle
cotton, sealing edges and top with UV medium
and paint
Photo courtesy of the artist

# 11. Wen Redmond
WWW.WENREDMOND.COM
NEW HAMPSHIRE, USA

"For *Leaping Point* I started with a photograph of a found bird's nest. I melded the photo with a fabric I had altered in Photoshop. The resulting digital fiber photograph was mounted onto sections of heavy stabilizer. Those segments were stitched and held together with a hand-tied book-binding method using dyed perle cotton.

"I did a series of these empty nests at the time my children were leaving home for college and jobs. It was only later that I realized I was working through this passage as a parent. Although it was a sad time, the process of creating this piece was joyful. My sadness drove me to make art, but it left me feeling satisfied. For me, art centers me, brings calm and perspective.

"For *Pause*, the photograph proper is a desaturated image of trees in the woods near me. I love being outside, taking pictures. At the time I made this piece, I was doing several different things with my photographs: one, I was manipulating them with my new sneaky layering technique, and two, I was printing on a new substrate—molding paste.

"I also used collage, which is a layering process I've enjoyed for years. I make actual collages, take photographs of them, and then layer them in Photoshop or other applications. The result is always a surprise. I was very excited. The energy created from that excitement carried me through to the end."

*When I finished this piece, I felt satisfied and happy. Also, thoughtful. I was thinking about how I could apply what I'd learned in a new and different way in my next project. That's a large part of my work—trying new things with my accumulated knowledge.*

Daryl Thetford. *Man in a Boat Alone*, 2016.
96" × 120".
Materials: 50-200 digitally collaged photographs,
aluminum, varnish
Techniques: digital collaging
Photo courtesy of the artist

Daryl Thetford. *Search for Reality*, 2016.
60" × 48".
Materials: 50-200 digitally collaged photographs,
aluminum, varnish
Techniques: digital collaging
Photo courtesy of the artist

# 12. Daryl Thetford
WWW.DARYLTHETFORD.COM
TENNESSEE, USA

"My wife and I were struggling with an issue she later wrote about for a *Psychology Today* magazine article. It was about envy of one's spouse's career. We were still happy together, but there were a lot of times when I felt very alone. During one of our conversations I told her I felt like a man in a boat alone. What I really wanted to express is the idea that ultimately, we are—each of us—alone.

*After I finished this piece, I felt a sense of satisfaction. Of course, it didn't rectify the situation between me and my wife, but I was very pleased with how the imagery seemed to evoke emotion in people who didn't know the story behind it. I found it was like a projection board. Some would talk about the loneliness it expressed, whereas others talked about its meditative quality.*

"For *Search for Reality* I was driving in a very rural area one night, listening to podcasts and receiving texts and Facebook messages, phone calls, and alerts from news organizations through my phone. I was struck by how, in this very rural place, I was still being bombarded with media. This, in turn, was contributing to my already great stress. I had an image of standing in front of a wall of media.

"I once heard Dave Matthews describe his songs as pretty dark and filled with pain, but his band puts a catchy melody behind it and suddenly people are dancing. I think my work, with my color choices, allows people to have the safety to acknowledge and connect to the work without being frightened by it, whereas if it was gray and black and brown, it would be scary, and people would not allow themselves to connect with it."

Ruth Ross. *Alien*, 2012. 4' × 5'.
Materials: acrylic on canvas
Techniques: painting
Photo by Dan Kvitka

# 13. Ruth Ross

RUTHROSSART@GMAIL.COM
OREGON, USA

The artist created *Alien* when she was going through chemotherapy.

"Being in my studio and painting was the way I escaped the exhaustion, anxiety, and discomfort that accompanied the treatment."

*After completion, there was a sense of satisfaction. Having expressed myself, I externalized what I was experiencing in such a way that others might be able to understand.*

*When you are immersed in a creative endeavor, you may find yourself in a meditative-like state in which your mind is able to relax. This is a step forward in your journey toward healing.*

Michelle Doll. *Melt 1*, 2012. 26″ × 33″.
Materials: oil, mylar, Plexiglas
Techniques: oil painting on mylar mounted on Plexiglas
Photo courtesy of Lyons Wier Gallery

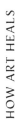

# 14. Michelle Doll
WWW.MICHELLEDOLL.COM
NEW JERSEY, USA

"*Melt 1* was inspired by an incident that happened to me in winter 2010, when I was violently mugged. During the attack, a feeling of calm came over me. I felt separated from my physical self and protected; I experienced what felt like an 'out of body experience,' where I left my body and was able to witness this incident as a viewer. And this feeling of clarity and empowerment gave me the bodily strength to fight my attacker."

*Since the incident, I have been seeking to reconnect with that feeling of inner calm and sense of safety through the practice of painting and meditation.*

· · · · · · · · · · · · · · · · · · · · · · · · · · · · · · ·

*When you are able to let go of emotional conflict, you are less bound by inner turmoil. Your mind is released so you can live your life with energy and pleasure.*

"The painting *Couple (LQ1)* was inspired by my own desire for care and compassionate connection. As a single mother, I was searching for ways to heal my heart by shifting my focus to the love and connection I so deeply longed for in an intimate relationship. In this painting, I was interested in capturing the transience between leaving and staying—that in-between state of conflict and desire. There is an intimate bond, yet a push and pull, that is physically and emotionally felt within a relationship."

*This painting was a transitional piece for me. It served to release the pain I felt so I could move forward in my understanding and search for positive relational connections.*

Michelle Doll. *Couple (LQ1)*, 2013. 50" × 44".
Materials: oil, canvas
Techniques: oil painting on canvas
Photo courtesy of Lyons Wier Gallery

Margaux Jacobs.
*8 Years Later*, 2017.
15" × 12".
Materials: acrylic paint
Techniques: painting
Photo courtesy of the artist

# 15. Margaux Jacobs
WWW.MARGAUXJACOBS.COM
FLORIDA, USA

"I created both *8 Years Later* and *Hold on My Dear* in reaction to and re-alization of what I had actually lost after eight years with an abusive boy-friend. While making these pieces, I was thinking how every time I look in the mirror, I see the years he added to my face. I lost my sense of self."

*When I finished these pieces, I released negative energy. I now have physical objects that hold the emotions and thoughts I was working through. I can put them down and walk away.*

*Anger and fear can torment us, fatigue us, and depress our spirits. Expressing these feelings can clear the way toward connection with what makes us content and happy.*

Margaux Jacobs. *Hold on My Dear*, 2016. 8″ × 12″.
Materials: acrylic paint, canvas
Techniques: painting
Photo courtesy of the artist

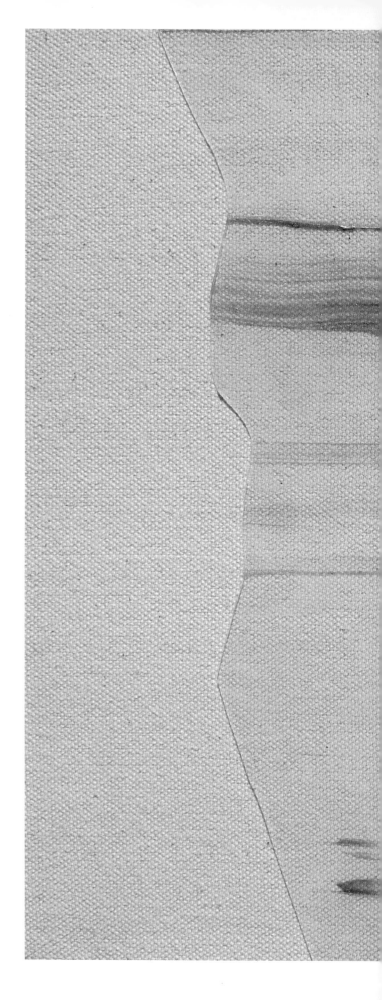

. . . . . . . . . . . . . . . . . . . . . . . . . . .

*The very act of
painting, sewing,
or shaping
clay to form a
representation of
a stress-producing
emotion can
actually release
that emotion from
your body, the
first step of the
healing process.*

106

Betsy Cole, *The Demons*, 2011. 20″ × 20″.
Materials: acrylic on canvas
Techniques: painting, brushwork
Photo courtesy of the artist

# 16. Betsy Cole
## WWW.BETSYCOLEART.COM
## COLORADO, USA

Part of a series of nine, *The Demons* came to Betsy in a moment of disquiet.

"I had been hard at work on my series Life Journey, composed of nine paintings, each depicting a powerful event, turning point, or insight into my life. Reliving events, applying paint to canvas, seeing bold visions of color appear before me—it was all much more exhausting than I'd anticipated.

"Needing a break, I joined friends and went to the theater. Although I don't recall the name of the play, I do remember coming home late and being angry and agitated. Never having painted in the dark of night, I went, however, directly to my studio and attacked a canvas. Like always, my work just spilled out without planning. In the morning, I saw the demons and knew they were the images that had been haunting me for so long."

*After painting* The Demons, *I had a huge sense of relief. But it wasn't until the next morning, when I first looked at my work, that I felt shock. I was shocked to see the darkness I'd expressed and felt, the pain it represented.*

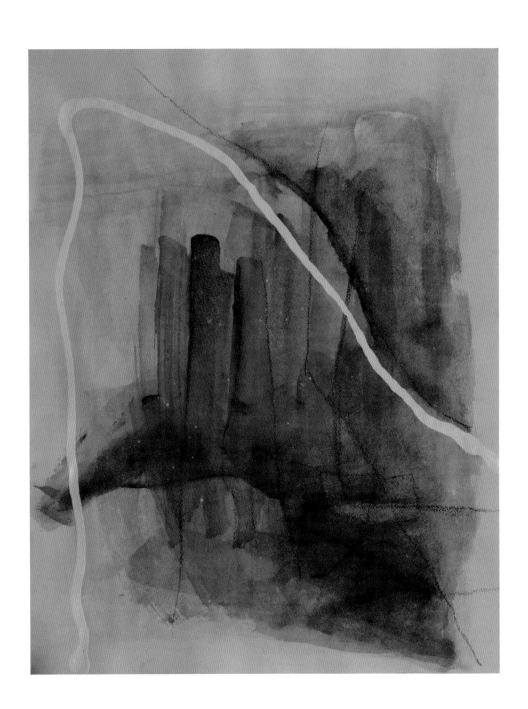

Ketty G. Devieux. *Fantasy on Paper*, 2017. 12″ × 16″.
Materials: gouache, ink, acrylic
Techniques: painting, brushstrokes
Photo courtesy of the artist

# 17. Ketty G. Devieux
WWW.KETTYDEVIEUX.COM
COLORADO, USA

*Fantasy on Paper* was created at a time when the artist was feeling great loneliness.

"My husband was often away for work for long periods, and my children, who were young adults, were living in two different states. I was approaching my sixtieth birthday. My constant loneliness felt absurd, and nothing in my life made much sense."

> *Creating* Fantasy on Paper *helped save me, as does all my art, from the pain of exile, of isolation, of self-doubt about my life choices. I left my home country nineteen years ago and have been dealing with these feelings ever since.*

Maren Cahill. *Flight*, 2018. 10″ × 20″. Materials: gallery-wrapped canvas, acrylic, paper, colored pencil, charcoal Techniques: collaging Photo courtesy of the artist

# 18. Maren Cahill
WWW.ARTICULATEARTS.COM
COLORADO, USA

Maren's work, *Flight*, began with a mental image of a woman falling through the predusk sky, her body collapsed inward. She didn't understand the meaning of this imagery but felt an urge to put it on paper. She started with the steep cliffs, surrendering to the process of following her instincts.

"I saw it in its totality and realized what it represented: after having lived and struggled with my mother's mental illness for years, I consciously chose to let go of my relationship with her. It suddenly became clear to me that, even though the choice to part ways was painful, I risked losing myself if I remained in her life. In the face of impending destruction—hers and mine—I chose flight instead. This was the most powerful transition of my life."

*After I realized the story* Flight *told, I was shaken to my core. I felt both humbled and empowered. It was as though a tremendous healing had just occurred. This piece somehow helped me spiritually to integrate my decision to reject the pain that had been overshadowing my life. I felt like I could now fly toward my own joy.*

Maxwell DeMulder. *Teatime*, 2017. 18" × 24".
Materials: charcoal, graphite, tea
Technique: drawing, tea-washing
Photo courtesy of the artist

# 19. Maxwell DeMulder
WWW.VISARTSCENTER.ORG/VISABILITY-GALLERY/
MARYLAND, USA

"I had recently survived a traumatic event around the time I joined the Visibility Art Lab. I always had tea when I was in the studio, which was a humanistic ritual to cope and deal with emotions from trauma. The skeleton reflects the hollowness I felt."

*For* Teatime, *the feelings were there and needed to be put down on paper. I felt a sense of acceptance, loss, and hope after completing this piece.*

Martin Wojnowski. *Keep Calm and Finish Your Tea, Darling*, 2017. 5' × 3'.
Materials: acrylic on canvas
Techniques: painting
Photo courtesy of the artist

# 20. Martin Wojnowski
WWW.MARTINWOJNOWSKI.COM
DUBAI, UAE

---

"*Keep Calm and Finish Your Tea, Darling* depicts the 'Old World' order, unprepared to face the new threats and oblivious to new dangers. The dangers come from climate change and inept politicians who risk their country's security by embarking on undeclared wars. I lost a relative on September 11. That event has changed the world. It is not safe and it's not predictable anymore. My painting is meant to convey the feeling of the 'calm before the storm.'

"I was driven to make this painting by frustration that the tragedies of past conflicts don't seem to inspire us to lead a more peaceful existence. Instead, they lead to greater tragedies that mostly affect innocent bystanders.

"After completing this piece, I've realized the futility of our reactions. Sometimes the only option to deal with trauma is to accept the fact that the event that caused it was beyond our control and "was meant to happen." Tragedy is part of the human experience."

*Let's be nice to each other, establish the right priorities, and consciously enjoy every moment.*

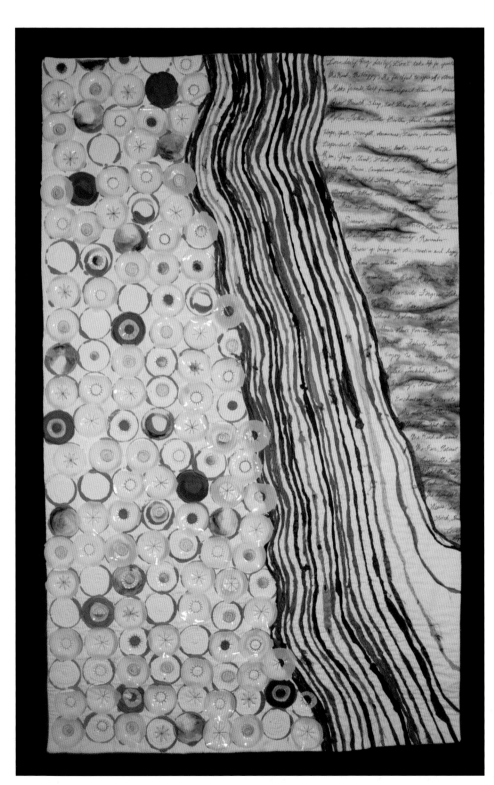

Mary Ann Vaca-Lambert. *Just a Whisper*, 2016. 39″ × 62″.
Materials: cotton fabric, silk fabric strands, cotton batting, Provox Extrabase plastic backing, thread, Inktense pigment blocks, writing brush, fabric paint
Techniques: free-motion quilting, couching, handwriting, drawing, painting, stamping
Photo courtesy of the artist

# 21. Mary Ann Vaca-Lambert

WWW.CLOTH2ART.COM

TEXAS, USA

In 2007, Mary Ann received a voice prosthesis that allows her to speak, but just above a whisper.

"I've come to understand and appreciate the subtleties of tone in the human voice, those little changes when one speaks, from a raise in pitch to an accentuated word. I've had to learn how to create these very common changes that other people take for granted. My prosthesis is made up of a tiny spool-shaped piece of plastic. It is set inside my throat. A plastic ring is the base that holds a 'button.' Together, the spool and button produce sound waves that enable me to speak. The plastic base has a backing that's a very thin plastic, much like the back of a Band-Aid, which I used in *Just a Whisper*.

"I created the work as I was going through a rollercoaster of emotions. On a daily basis, I found that strangers made unkind comments about my voice. I had to work through feelings of hurt and anger. I felt demeaned and offended. It was hurtful to be struggling to speak, only to have someone tell me what a horrible voice I had or that the sounds I was making were horrible or that I sounded terrible. Some would ask, 'What happened to you?' The indignity I felt was the catalyst for making *Just a Whisper*.

"While I worked on *Just a Whisper*, I was thinking about my experience. As I attached the plastic rings that hold my speaking button on my throat to the foundation cloth, I thought about the transformation I've been through. When I created a representation of "sound waves," using silk yarn remnants to depict how my voice is created both artificially and naturally, I felt grateful for the miracle of science. The process of creating this piece turned out to be one of the most rewarding accomplishments of my life. Although I had intended to write the mean and painful things that had been said to me, I realized that I wanted, rather, to concentrate on thoughts of hope, happiness, thankfulness, and joy. I want to live by these and maintain a positive outlook, with gratitude, about my journey."

Liz Alpert Fay. *I.C.U.*, 2016. 93" × 84" × 64" (installation).
Materials for wall piece: wool on linen, hand-hooked; "brass" (on floor): mixed
materials, hand-hooked on linen
Techniques: needle-punching, embroidering
Photo by Brad Stanton

# 22. Liz Alpert Fay
WWW.LIZALPERTFAY.COM
CONNECTICUT, USA

Liz resides in Sandy Hook, a community that experienced a horrific mass shooting at their elementary school.

"On December 14, 2012, twenty first-grade students and six adults were killed. A military-style assault weapon enabled the shooter to kill them in just five minutes. Because of their capacity to kill, these guns have been used in many other mass shootings throughout the country."

*The pain and sadness I felt about Sandy Hook will never go away. But as an artist, I feel making art is my way to speak out. I hope to reach more and more people each time I show this work,* I.C.U.

Liz's piece *Autumn Garden* is a testament to her love of the season.

"It's my favorite. I love the colors, the harvesting of vegetables, and the cold, crisp air. One day, as I was walking down the back steps of my house, I was surprised to see there were flowers hiding in a pile of leaves, nestled in my garden. The vibrant colors of the asters and chrysanthemums were shouting out."

*When the snow comes, I'll be hoping for an early spring—the bright green of new shoots—and a birth of a new generation. This piece represents that hope.*

*Ring of Fire* is based on a photograph the artist took of a weathered fence post on a beach in Michigan.

Liz Alpert Fay. *Ring of Fire*, 2009. 32″ × 46″ (size of hooked piece).
Materials: hand-dyed wool on linen
Techniques: hand-hooking (cut wool strips removed from the center of the hooked piece lie beneath, on the floor)
Photo by Brad Stanton

"I loved that the tree rings were visible and even enhanced by both time and the elements. When this piece was still in the design stages, forest fires were spreading rampantly in California. I happened to see a TV news program in which the commentator described how burning a ring of fire around an undisturbed area of vegetation is a system to bring raging fires under control."

*This piece symbolizes hope. It shows that even in the midst of death and destruction, there is still beauty to be found.*

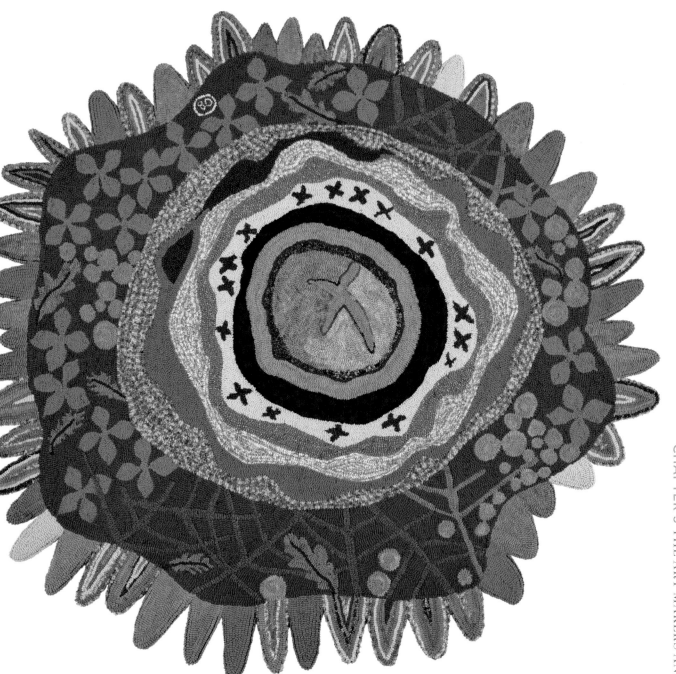

Liz Alpert Fay. *Autumn Garden*, 2009. 48" × 53".
Materials: hand-dyed and recycled wool on linen
Techniques: hand-hooking
Photo by Brad Stanton

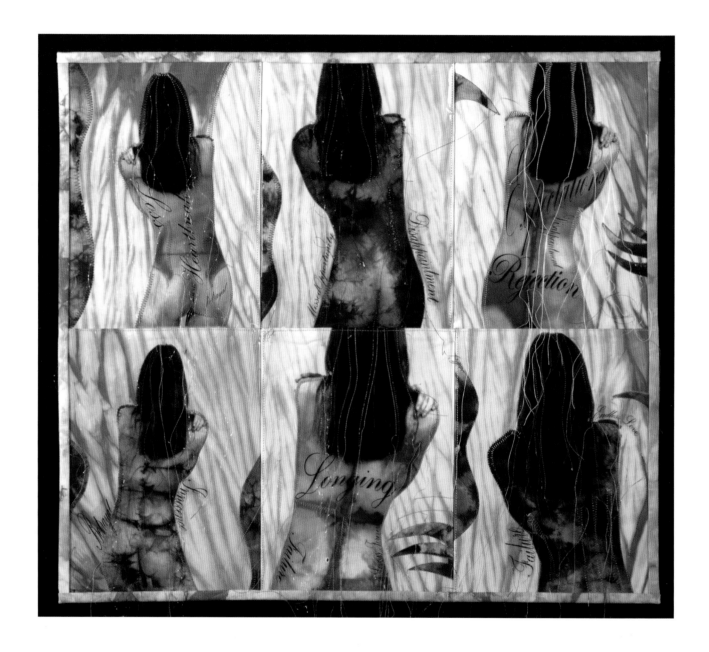

Patricia Kennedy-Zafred. *Back At It*, 2011. 25.5″ × 21.5″.
Materials: acetate, hand-dyed fabric, vinyl, rayon, cotton and metallic thread, batting
Technique: art quilting
Photo by Larry Berman

# 23. Patricia Kennedy-Zafred
WWW.PATTYKZ.COM
PENNSYLVANIA, USA

Patricia created *Back At It* after having been away from her art studio for eleven years.

"When my employer retired, the lure to return to making art presented itself. This piece was a reflection of facing my doubts, insecurities, and fears. Could I make art again? Would it be successful? Would I enjoy it? *Back At It* posed this question: Should I find another professional position or choose art and face the demons in my studio?"

> *When I finished this piece, I felt a sense of relief and satisfaction that I was able to express what I was feeling. The work allowed me to let go of the issues. I left them in the piece.*

"I created the series *Tagged* to tell a story about a shameful period in American history not often acknowledged. The motivation started with one photograph: the image of a mother carrying her baby, both with tags pinned to their clothing. It was a mystery to me when I first discovered it online. It turns out it was taken during the two-week period when innocent Japanese Americans living on the West Coast were forced from their homes into internment camps as a result of Executive Order 9066.

"My series reflects on the unfair judgments made about people on the basis of culture, religion, language, or the color of their skin. This kind of judgment continues to take place even today across our country.

"I obtained some of the images I used for the silkscreens from the Library of Congress, and others from a university library. Further research provided me with the names of the children, and their tags in my quilts reflect their actual names and the location of the camps they were sent to. In one of the images, a mother and her baby could not be identified until 2014, when the daughter, now an adult, contacted me with her mother's name, Fumiko Hayashida. She died at the age of 103."

*Telling this story was satisfying because it's only recently that this dark chapter in American history has been revealed and reported on in detail. Several museums have been created at the sites of the internment camps since. But working on these pieces also made me sad, staring into the innocent faces every day. Yet, I felt an obligation to tell their story and was satisfied I was able to do it in a beautiful and compelling way. In retrospect, I think it's my best work.*

Patricia Kennedy-Zafred. *Tagged*, 2015. 60" × 45".
Materials: hand-silk-screened images on hand-dyed fabric, image transfer
techniques (lettering and tag information), fusing, discharge
Techniques: appliquéing, machine-piecing, quilting
Photo by Larry Berman

Colleen Ansbaugh. *Injection Site*, 2017. 24″ × 30″.
Materials: cotton fabric, netting, paint
Technique: hand-dyeing, silk-screening, hand- and machine-quilting, painting
Photo courtesy of the artist

# 24. Colleen Ansbaugh
WWW.COLLEENANSBAUGH.COM
WISCONSIN, USA

The artist created *Injection Site* to visualize the injection process as the needle enters the body.

"A coworker had a foot, then leg, and subsequently her other leg amputated due to diabetes. It was difficult to watch her decline, although her spirit remained positive. I now understand injections for diabetes become painful and difficult to administer as sites become overly used and scar tissue develops. The location of the next injection can become a challenge."

*As I created this piece, I felt concern for those with diabetes. For me, it was a relief to work through my feelings about the idea of living with pain.*

Colleen created *In Search* to help her explore the idea of mortality.

"I wanted it to show the transition of the inner spirit from the body upward to heaven. I tapped into thoughts and prayers during the passage of both my parents and brother. They all died within a very short time of one another."

In Search *brought temporary emotional relief, although grieving came much later.*

"*Riverbed* stands for the river of emotions that always come up for me at Christmastime. There's the wonderful joy associated with my religious beliefs combined with the passing of loved ones. It is a bittersweet time of year for me."

*Completing this piece felt satisfying. It represents how the season's colors flow together, the sights and sounds, all come together to bring on a strong emotion of hope and gratitude.*

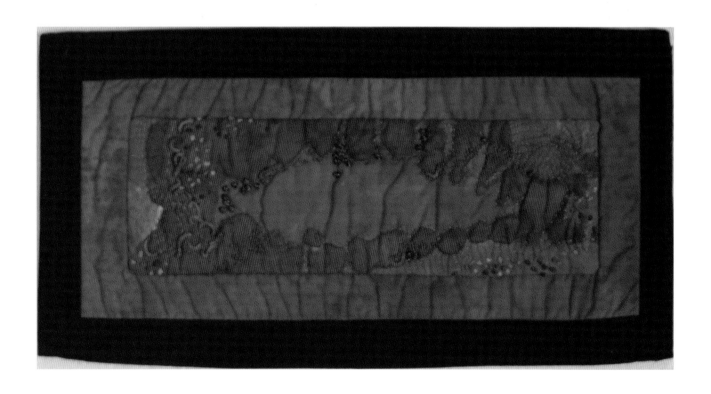

Colleen Ansbaugh. *Riverbed*, 2014. 9" × 18".
Materials: cotton fabric, batting
Techniques: hand-dyeing, hand- and machine-embroidering, quilting
Photo courtesy of the artist

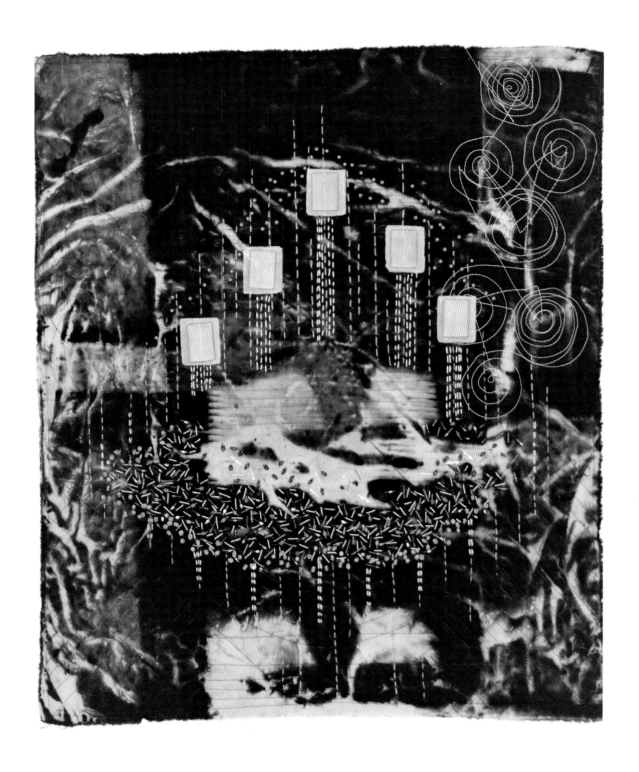

Colleen Ansbaugh. *In Search*, 2018. 24″ × 24″.
Materials: cotton fabric
Techniques: silk-screening, hand- and machine-stitching
Photo courtesy of the artist

Line Dufour. *Excitement* (Well Being series),
2008. 60" × 30".
Materials: wool, assorted yarns
Techniques: tapestry, hand-weaving
Photo courtesy of the artist

Line Dufour. *Gratitude* (Well
Being series), 2009. 60" × 15".
Materials: assorted yarns
Techniques: tapestry,
hand-weaving
Photo courtesy of the artist

# 25. Line Dufour
WWW.LINEDUFOUR.COM
ONTARIO, CANADA

Line created her Well Being series to inspire positive feelings in those who see the work.

"Feelings are universal. We all have them. To deny one's feelings and the feelings of others is toxic.

"With the Well Being series, including *Excitement* and *Gratitude*, I hope that when the viewer looks at these pieces, the colors of each of the chakras will help make them feel more whole, create a sense of well-being, excitement, joy, love, gratitude—a state of happiness.

"The Well Being series documented my journey to achieve health in all areas of life by coming to terms with my own human nature, filled with positive and negative feelings. Being in touch with all of one's feelings is the key to well-being and wholeness; it enables us to live an authentic life, a life in which we can honor our multidimensionality."

*The colors in the Well Being series were inspired by the colors used to describe the chakras. In Hinduism, these are energy centers that are tied to certain areas of the physical body. The goal is to keep all of the chakras in balance. We must take responsibility for living a balanced life.*

Susan Brooks. *Daisy*, 2018. 26.5" × 71".
Materials: cotton, thickened dyes
Techniques: cotton mono-printing with thickened
dyes, raw-edge appliquéing, machine-stitching,
hand-stitching of words based on a poem by April
Hill in *Too Much Time, Women in Prison* by Jane
Evelyn Atwood
Photo courtesy of the artist

Susan Brooks. *Reality*, 2011. 31.5" × 54.5".
Materials: cotton, thickened dyes, thread
Techniques: cotton mono-printing with thickened
dyes, machine-stitching
Photo courtesy of the artist

# 26. Susan Brooks

SUSANBROOKSTEXTILEARTIST.COM
COLORADO, USA

"I volunteered at a women's prison and met a woman named Daisy there. I created *Daisy* after she shared her life story of going from anger and violence over her abusive past—to freedom. As she told her story, she told me she pictured Jesus circling in a helicopter over the facility, beckoning for everyone to become His daughters. He clothed them in gowns and tiaras, freeing them with His love.

"I was inspired to create *Daisy* as I listened to the emotions Daisy expressed. I felt like I experienced her freedom while listening to her story, watching her facial expressions go from despair to joy.

"*Daisy* was my attempt to represent a woman in prison and the value of her life despite her circumstances. We so often pass the homeless, mentally ill, abused, and poor in the street and not realize their humanity and their need for the same basic securities that we all want. Each of these pieces was a combination of the joy of getting emotions onto canvas, but also frustration because I wanted to go back and perfect my work.

"*Reality* represents the need for women to find their self-worth based on their own strengths, talents, and achievements, rather than looking for the approval and acceptance of others."

*I created this piece based on my daughter's book of poetry,* Rush of Water, *by Chara DeWolf. The poems are about discovering one's own value in the world. I created twenty-three pieces based on it. All my works are meant to tell a healing story, hopefully touching the heart of viewers so they might experience their own healing.*

Jóh Ricci. *Entangled Flight*, 2014. 5" × 7" × 7".
Materials: fine nylon thread, rayon and cotton
yarn, Japanese paper, magazine clippings,
locust tree thorns
Techniques: knotting
Photo courtesy of the artist

# 27. Jóh Ricci

JOHRICCI.EMBARQSPACE.COM
PENNSYLVANIA, USA

The artist created a series of three vessels, reflecting a transition in relationships, life, and a time filled with challenges, struggles, and decisions.

"*Entangled Flight* reflects inspiration drawn from nature. The organic form sits on top of a wooden stand, almost nestlike. Inside, a lone bluebird is subtle and almost invisible along with words of thoughts and emotions, where sharp and painful thorns generate a feeling of entrapment and isolation."

*I always have a sense of accomplishment with each piece I create. With this series, there was a sense of temporary relief, a new intensity, and new beginnings.*

Chizu Kago. *Beginning*, 2017.
11″ × 9″ × 7″.
Materials: windmill palm
Techniques: basketry
Photo courtesy of the artist

Chizu Kago. *Wound*, 2016.
11″ × 7″ × 5″.
Materials: windmill palm
Techniques: basketry
Photo courtesy of the artist

# 28. Chizu Kago
HTTPS://CHIZU-BASKETRY.JIMDO.COM/
CHIZU-SEKIGUCHI-WORKS
SHIZUOKA, JAPAN

"*Beginning* represents the state of the plant when its root is in the soil and is sucking up water and nourishment. It is trying to sprout out of the ground and be born into the world."

*For me, this was a thing of great joy to create.*

"My piece *Wound* expresses conflict I have felt. It represents a desire to endure despite having had a wound to my heart."

*This was an important piece for me because it tells of a need to endure.*

* * * * * * * * * * * * * * * * * * * * * * * * * *

*Creating art teaches you to understand your own inner language.*

Chiako Dosho. *Cherry Blossom 1*, 2001. 6.5″ × 6.5″.
Materials: Japanese old kimono (silk, wool), embroidery thread
Techniques: stitching, quilting
Photo courtesy of the artist

# 29. Chiako Dosho
WWW.CHIAKODOSHOART.COM
KANAGAWA-KEN, JAPAN

"When I have been hurt deeply, and my art is about that pain, the feeling behind the work grows deeper. When there is great joy, it appears in the colors and the depth of the work.

"All of my work reflects my heart, including *Cherry Blossom 1*. Even though the meaning will be different for everyone who sees the art, as long as someone feels something, that is all that matters."

*I always struggle with a lot of problems and face obstacles when I make art. I understand most of the troubles will not be solved. Still, art for me is rehabilitation. No matter how hard it is, I can forget about the time while I am concentrating on my art.*

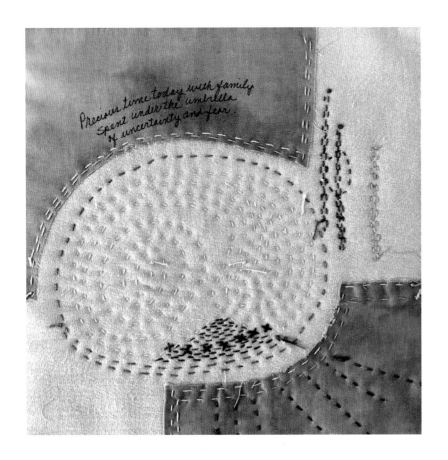

Carole Frocillo. *Waiting Game Day 1*, 2018. 8" × 8".
Materials: commercial, hand-dyed, and surface-designed fabric; thread
Techniques: raw-edge hand-appliquéing, surface designing, stitching
Photo courtesy of the artist

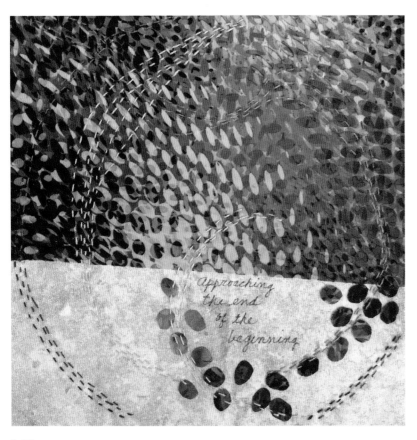

Carole Frocillo. *Day 12*, 2018. 8" × 8".
Materials: commercial, hand-dyed, and surface-designed fabric; thread
Techniques: raw-edge hand-appliquéing, surface designing, stitching
Photo courtesy of the artist

# 30. Carole Frocillo
WWW.CAROLEANNFROCILLO.COM
CALIFORNIA, USA

"My family has a long history of breast cancer. Every year, I approach my breast screening with trepidation but have been able to take a huge sigh of relief. Again, in 2017, the technician said, on first look, that I was fine. My daughter, on the other hand, had her own mammogram a day after mine—and she was *not* fine. My first thought through the tears was *Why her? Why not me?* But, thankfully, her cyst removal was clean.

"The next day, I received a call saying that I needed to return for more testing, that I had an unusual and suspicious arrangement of calcifications. I would need general anesthesia, which required pre-op screening. That screening indicated that something was wrong with my heart. The cancer surgery was canceled until the heart issue could be addressed.

"Eventually, the cancer surgery was completed. It had taken longer than expected because they had to remove tissue in increments until the margins were clear. I couldn't seem to quiet myself internally. Finally, I went to my studio and made the first piece of what became a series. Each day, for nineteen days, I created a piece based on my feelings that day.

"I am a person who is used to being in charge. I no longer felt in charge. I am a caregiver by nature. This new role of needing to accept care made me uncomfortable

"For these pieces, I chose hand stitching because of its imperfect look and because it was important to me to be in charge. At the end of the three- or four-hour sessions it took to make each piece, I felt relieved and in control. These days, each time I look at the pieces collectively, I see and feel the fear, the humor, the waiting, and the love and support from my family. By challenging myself in this way, I gained strength and found a sense of purpose during this difficult time of waiting."

Susan Else. *Hope*, 2016. 15″ × 12″ × 12″.
Materials: fabric, metal armature, yarn, thread
Techniques: collaging and quilting cloth over armature
Photo courtesy of Marty McGillivray

# 31. Susan Else
WWW.SUSANELSE.COM
CALIFORNIA, USA

"The figure in *Hope* has a surface reminiscent of cracked earth, and she's kneeling in a dry riverbed. A small green seedling grows out of her hand. I was thinking about how, in dire situations, hope can be an expression of will, something we pull from inside ourselves to survive."

Susan notes that although she likes to include a whimsical element in her work, lately she's been having trouble doing so.

"My work has become less humorous as the world has turned."

*After completing* Hope, *I felt grim but determined. Like many other people, I'm having a hard time seeing a way through these troubled times.*

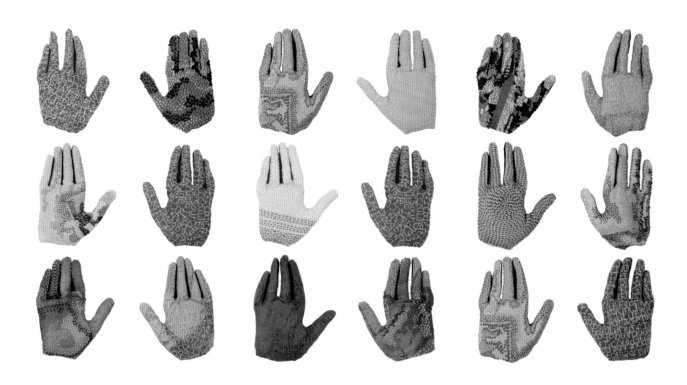

Stewart Kelly. *40 Hands*, 2018. Forty textile sculptures, approx. 6″ × 4.7″ (each).
Materials: hand-dyed indigo cotton and silk fabric, cotton thread, ribbon
Techniques: hand-dyeing, hand- and machine-embroidering
Photo courtesy of the artist

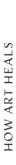

# 32. Stewart Kelly
STEWARTKELLYARTIST.COM
MANCHESTER, UK

Stewart is an artist whose current practice lies at the intersection of art, health, and well-being. He recently completed a project called Body Mapping. The project consists of a series of textile sculptures that incorporate text, stitch, and dye.

"The pieces are based on the idea that art can be transformational. It is important that we reflect upon our experiences and consider how they affect us.

"The work *40 Hands* consists of forty textile sculptures of my hands. The pieces were constructed individually from indigo-dyed cotton and silk cloth and later embellished with hand and machine embroidery.

"I wanted to create a piece of work over a long period of time as a way of documenting the range of my experienced emotions. The hands were physically demanding to create, an appropriate metaphor for the trials of any creative journey."

*Stitching, by nature, is slow and reflective, offering opportunities to daydream. Turning forty, I wanted time to reflect on the past, both personally and professionally. Upon completion, I felt a sense of achievement. It signified the end of one chapter and the beginning of a new one.*

Stewart Kelly. *Face to Face 7*, 2017. 7.5' × 1.6'.
Materials: ink, paper, thread
Techniques: drawing, collaging, machine embroidering
Photo courtesy of the artist

"My Face to Face series was completed between 2015 and 2017. There are eleven works that developed from previous projects and focused on an abstract interpretation of the human form. The Face to Face series is intentionally more figurative and confrontational in its appearance than my other works. It was also an opportunity to explore color.

"The pieces were constructed in several stages. Initially, I made several observational studies of faces from life, using ink on paper. I then cut out all the faces and began to arrange them in the form of a collage. Finally, I machine-stitched over the surface to enhance lines and blend colors.

"I was interested in creating a series that is neither exclusively drawings nor textiles. Therefore, the pieces are ambiguous in both the process and subject matter, exploring the effects of overlaying multiple images. These layers of different materials and processes create images that seek to achieve a deliberate ambiguity, giving rise to the many possibilities of interpretation. The viewer is encouraged to consider where one process ends and another begins."

*The layers of drawn and stitched lines recorded an accumulation of observations and mapped encounters. The pieces are complex and were intense in their construction. Face to Face 7 was completed approximately halfway through the project. It marked the point at which the pieces began to increase significantly in scale. On completing the piece, I felt a sense of relief, yet also achievement.*

Stewart Kelly. *Face to Face 7* (detail). Photo courtesy of the artist

Tien Chiu. *Bipolar Disorder: Inside the Prison of my Mind*, 2016. 27" × 21".
Materials: silk, nylon, mercerized cotton, unmercerized cotton, cotton batting
Techniques: handweaving
Photo courtesy of the artist

# 33. Tien Chiu
WWW.TIENCHIU.COM
CALIFORNIA, USA

"I have bipolar disorder, and it has almost killed me twice: first, because the agonizing pain of bipolar depression nearly drove me to suicide. The second way was more insidious: the social stigma against people with mental illness kept me from talking about it openly for many years.

"When I finally decided to 'come out' about having bipolar disorder, I was surprised by the response. Shortly after I posted my story on my blog, people started emailing me to share their own experience—friends and family members of people with mental illness, or people grappling with it themselves. Many of them thanked me for having the courage to share my struggle. One person said simply, 'It made it much easier for me to know that I am not alone.'

"Thankfully, my medical team and I have found the right combination of medications to keep my mood stable, and my life is no longer in danger. But as someone who has chosen to be 'out' about having bipolar disorder, I think it's vital for me to speak out, to help put a human face on mental illness. Only then can we end the stigma."

Bipolar Disorder: Inside the Prison of my Mind *expresses my struggle with mental illness. Before being diagnosed and treated for bipolar disorder, I often felt locked into my own head, trapped in a chaos of shifting moods. These are represented by swaths of blue for deep depression and patches of orange, evoking the fires of mania.*

Jackie Abrams. *The Blues Sisters*, 2017. 9.5" × 7" and 1.5" × 6.5".
Materials: cotton and rice papers, acrylic paint and media, wire, waxed linen
thread, ribbon, beads
Techniques: basketry, painting, embellishing
Photo by Al Karevy

# 34. Jackie Abrams

WWW.JACKIEABRAMS.COM
VERMONT, USA

"*The Blues Sisters* are part of an ongoing series, Women Forms, which is a collection of woven vessels that speak of women, their shared stories, and their layers of experience, formed and shaped by society. The interiors of the vessels catch the light in unexpected ways, a reflection of the inner strengths of women—strengths not always visible. *The Blues Sisters* stand together and gather strength from their mutual support.

"My craft development work with women in Africa during many trips from 2005 to 2009 had a profound influence on this series. I try to reflect what I learned from these women, from being in Africa, and from experiencing a different life and culture."

> *The completion of each piece allowed me to step back, take a deep breath, and think about what would come next.*

"I made my first plastic bag coiled basket while working in Pokuase, Ghana, teaching the women to crochet saleable items by using recycled plastic bags. As they practiced their crocheting, I started to coil. I continue to coil, transforming silk blouses, handmade papers, and other materials into vessels that speak of these women.

"*Stone Stories* is from my Spirit Women series. The technique is an adaptation of the ancient technique of coiling. I use recycled materials, leaving the cores exposed, and each stitch connects and reinforces the row that came before. The stones represent our stories, stories that shape our lives. They become both our strengths and our weaknesses and make us who we are. They may be spoken or unspoken, seen or unseen."

*In many ways, the audience's response to my work is what has become most important. I want people to "know" these are women, that they are all different and that they all matter.*

· · · · · · · · · · · · · · · · · · · · · · · · · · · · · · · · · · · · · · · · · · · · · · · ·

*Art adapts to every imaginable problem, heightening one's power to find insight and, ultimately, transformation.*

Jackie Abrams. *Stone Stories*, 2013. 9" × 6" × 6".
Materials: plastic newspaper bags, waxed linen thread, stones
Techniques: basketry, stitching
Photo by Al Karevy

Liz Ackert. *Mended Heart*, 2014. 3.5" × 3" × 1".
Materials: Atlantic heart cockle (*Dinocardium robustum*) from Avon, North Carolina; cotton embroidery floss; overdyed fragment of vintage silk
Techniques: off-loom weaving
Photo courtesy of the artist

Liz Ackert. *Mended Heart* (back).
Photo courtesy of the artist

# 35. Liz Ackert
WWW.IMGOINGTOTEXAS.HOME.BLOG
TEXAS, USA

"Two months after my mom passed away, I began to collect broken shells rather than perfect ones. Perhaps they were a metaphor.

"Six years later, I was trying to break free of my precise stitching style and signed up for a class with Jude Hill at Spirit Cloth. Because the focus was on weaving with nontraditional looms, I decided to 'mend' one of the shells as a tribute.

"After creating a warp over the hole in the shell, I found myself tearing out one woven iteration after another. My inner critic continuously chanted, 'Not good enough, not good enough,' until at last I ended up with a perfectly plain, meticulously worked patch over the broken exterior. It was the epitome of my old modus operandi. Mom would have loved it.

"But it wasn't really what *I* wanted to do. It was too perfect. So, I tore a thin strip from a pink silk scarf, threaded it on a needle, and began to weave it back and forth on the interior of the shell. As I neared the end, the silk became hopelessly tangled in the warp.

"Beginning to cut through the weaving yet again, I suddenly stopped and nudged down some of the threads. A heart revealed itself—torn and tattered. It was better than 'good enough.'"

Mended Heart *marked a turning point. Thereafter, I traded the precision of carefully counted threads for the wild mind of patch-play and spontaneous stitching and never looked back.*

Bonnie J. Smith. *Swimming Upstream*, 2012. 65″ × 35″.
Materials: Kona cottons, wool, polyester batting, thread
Techniques: machine-stitching
Photo by Spring Mountain Gallery

# 36. Bonnie J. Smith
WWW.BONNIEJOFIBERARTS.COM
CALIFORNIA, USA

"When I created *Swimming Upstream*, I had been thinking for years about how to tell the story of the work injury that forced me to use a wheelchair. Swimming every day, I would think about how to let others know about the journey I had taken.

"The injury was almost ten years behind me, but the mental anguish still had a hold on me. Creating the textile artwork lifted those feelings off my shoulders. I had been seeing a psychiatrist for years to help with my feelings, but physically creating the designs—and touching the fabrics—put the entire experience on the outside of my physical body.

"When *Swimming Upstream* was finished, and I sat back and looked at the work on my design wall, I realized the work was not just my story to tell; it belongs to anyone with a similar story. Emotionally, we are all together."

*I felt such joy when the work was completed that I literally shouted it from the rooftop. I showed the work to curators, other artist, and doctors. I knew I had tapped a vein of breakthrough for myself.*

"When I viewed a photograph of myself floating along in the water, I knew this work needed to be made. This is how I create most of my artwork; I look at a picture I have taken or hear someone's story and know that I must let the world know about this story.

"With *Contemplate #9*, I knew in my artistic career this piece was a milestone. First, the work was aesthetically wonderful to look at, but it also shows me contemplating my life and thinking about what was next in my personal journey.

"I believe we should spend more time contemplating—taking stock of our lives, thinking about what is around the corner, and thinking about what we can do to make our lives more complete and fulfilling."

*I felt tremendous satisfaction when this work was finished. It really did make me think about my future and the direction I wanted my life to take. We can heal and make space for ourselves in this world.*

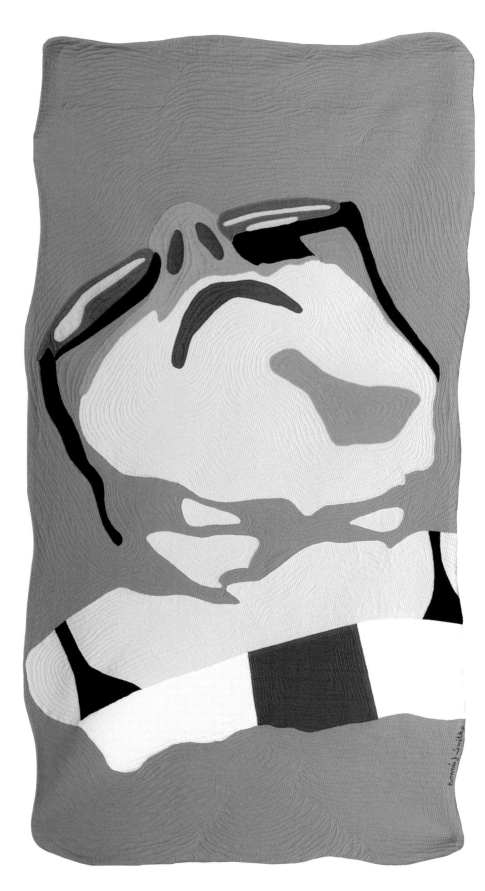

Bonnie J. Smith.
*Contemplate #9*,
65" × 35".
Materials: Kona
cottons, wool, polyes-
ter batting, thread
Techniques:
machine-stitching
Photo by Spring
Mountain Gallery

Ane Lyngsgaard. *My Scandinavian Roots*, 2019. 2′ × 2′ × 2.9′.
Materials: willow, bark, fiber, concrete
Techniques: weaving
Photo courtesy of the artist

# 37. Ane Lyngsgaard
## WWW.PILERIET.DK
## HOERNING, DENMARK

"I have been weaving organic asymmetric baskets for some years. In the beginning, it was a question about shape, balance, and beauty, but even after mastering those skills, I could not let them go. I kind of fell in love with them, and I had an inner urge to continue to make them, no matter if I was busy with other kinds of basketry.

"After making maybe thirty, I realized I was weaving myself into every basket. It was about my femininity, and it was about stretching the empty space inside the baskets so the empty space could fill with energy. It was about being balanced and whole and beautiful!

"As a child, I was sexually abused from the ages of three to six. In different ways, it made my life difficult, and I went through therapy as a young adult—thankfully. Even with therapy, though, I somehow always felt something had been damaged inside me."

*Weaving baskets, including* My Scandinavian Roots, *often brings me into a meditative area without words. Making these organic baskets gave me an inner experience of an undamaged femininity, of being beautiful despite what happened to me. I realize I was working on energizing the empty space inside me. I was working on being balanced even though I saw myself as kind of asymmetric inside. I was working on a feminine energy coming from the earth. It was beautiful, and it was mine! Working with these baskets gave me, at last, acceptance of the person I am.*

Irene Manion. *Death and Transfiguration*, 2011. 3′ × 1.8′.
Materials: satin polyester, rayon and polyester thread
Techniques: dye sublimation-printing onto satin polyester, machine-embroidering, appliquéing
Photo courtesy of the artist

# 38. Irene Manion
WWW.IRENEMANION.COM
NEW SOUTH WALES, AUSTRALIA

"Losing one's mother is a devastating event, and for me, it was a most painful and prolonged period of sadness. The pain remained raw and prominent in my mind, and the passage of time did little to soften my profound feelings of loss.

"My mother's northern European background was one where hands-on crafts such as weaving, knitting, and crocheting were an intrinsic part of daily life and an expression of traditional culture. We practiced these crafts together as a family throughout my entire childhood and beyond.

"At the time of her death, I had been working on a textile series that was based on urban bird life, and I was challenged by a new arrival on the local scene: the richly colored rainbow lorikeet. Trying to depict this exquisite bird's joyous personality and its rainbow plumage into designs was a challenge that I had been exploring across several pieces.

"After my mother's death, I felt compelled to transform my subject matter in ways that reflected my bereavement. My colorful birds would need to be depicted without color, as my mother's death had taken the color from my own life, and the pain dulled and leached my vitality.

"In the textile piece *Death and Transfiguration*, the animated lorikeet in the top left-hand corner looks back at me in a last farewell glance. In the bottom right-hand corner, the 'transfigured' lorikeet is now white and hangs lifelessly upside down, with a more stylized appearance. The background resembles a woven tapestry in the colors of the lorikeet. It is a trompe l'oeil surface, created digitally, with a very stylized lorikeet motif patterned on it, as though the color that has been drained from the lifeless bird reemerges or bleeds into in the colored tapestry.

"The imagery for *Death and Transfiguration* was digitally designed and then dye-sublimated onto fabric. The appliquéd pieces were stitched using my self-developed 'long-stitch' technique."

*By directly confronting the subject of my mother's death through imagery, I was forced to analyze my emotions in detail. Completion of the piece helped me work through my memories of my intense childhood experiences and my deep friendship with my mother. I was able to come to terms with the finality of death and was forced to bring my mind to a confrontation with the permanence of death as being something that I could bear by carrying my love for her with me and using it to feed into my daily existence in a positive way.*

Irene Manion. *Death and Transfiguration* (detail).
Photo courtesy of the artist

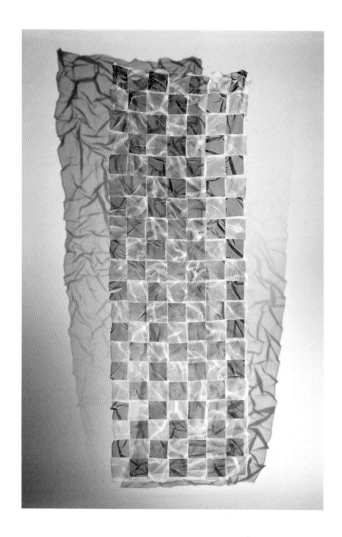

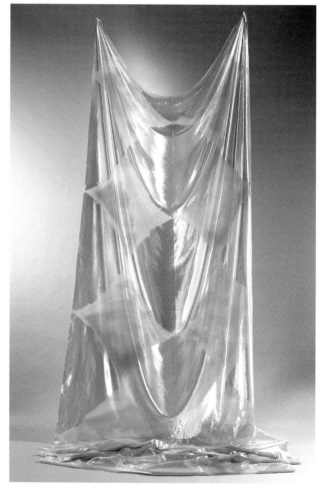

Junco Sato Pollack. *SKY/SKY* from the Sky/Cloud series (1995–2006), 2003. 103″ × 40″.
Materials: polyester organza
Techniques: heat-compressing, digital imaging and heat-printing, dye-sublimating on polyester organza
Photo courtesy of the artist

Junco Sato Pollack. *Sky/Cloud #2*, 2003. 15″ × 60″.
Materials: disperse dyes on metallic polyester organza
Techniques: melting off, Devore voiding, *shibori*, digital imaging, heat transfer printing
Photo courtesy of the artist

# 39. Junco Sato Pollack
WWW.JUNCOSATOPOLLACK.COM
GEORGIA, USA

"Born and raised in Japan, I was introduced to Buddhism early in my life. More or less, Buddhism formed my cultural and spiritual background. I was also a dancer at a young age (six to fifteen years of age), studying modern dance under a Buddhist monk and his wife who inherited an old Buddhist temple and built in it a dance studio near my hometown. They had been professional dancers in Tokyo and returned to this town to continue operating the studio.

"I traveled weekly by train to the studio, and soon I was selected to join the dance troupe that presented performances in art centers in the region. I enjoyed traveling on the train and dancing, which gave me an eye and perception for kinetic movements inspired by nature—trees, grass, birds, air, and so on.

"I moved to the United States in 1973 and eventually moved to Atlanta, Georgia, in 1992. I was awestruck by the southern sun and blue sky. I began photographing the sky and, after capturing more than 2,000 images, contemplated the paradox that to photograph blue sky as an image, I had to include a cloud formation within the view. This realization came like a moment of a new Zen Koan: Can you photograph Emptiness? The answer is yes, but there has to be a Void in the Emptiness to distinguish the two.

"The philosophy of Zen, the teaching set forth by Zen master D. T. Suzuki during the 1950s in New York, greatly influenced American abstract painters who integrated the phenomenon of accident and chance into the process of making art. I met and studied with Zen master Keido Fukushima in Atlanta and in Kyoto around this time. Zen master Keido Fukushima, who was a master calligrapher as well, studied under Suzuki as a student in Kyoto.

"It all made perfect sense to me and informed my vision for the next series that I produced between 1995 and 2006: the Sky/Cloud series. In that body of work, I expressed Heart Sutra chanting in terms of kinetic shapes, color blocks, and vibrations. The premise of this work is that the idea of color is an illusion, just as the sky is an emptiness that appears as if it exists but is only a construct of the mind.

"These works were produced by integrating handwork, machine work, modern technology, and chance and include a large-scale, fabric-based sculptural kinetic installation. I frequented a digital print studio in Canada to use an industrial roller heat-transfer printing machine and wide-format digital printer.

"Having built my art studio by the lake in the foothills of the mountains, I was surrounded by beautiful and pure nature while creating the series, allowing me to contemplate the meaning of art and living, and to be one with art and nature. It was a most rewarding period of my creative life, and spiritually nurturing.

"I was taking a walk on the beach at sunset, my usual daily afternoon walk, and on the third consecutive day, on the same section of the beach, I encountered a gray heron. I would walk toward it, come close, and then it would fly farther down the beach. This gently paced chase went on for three days. I wondered why. Then I realized that the heron must be waiting for something or someone. There was a sense of longing and persistence in the bird's demeanor.

"The next day at sunset, sure enough, I saw two gray herons enjoying the serene beach. The newly arrived heron was slightly smaller, and together they provided the yin and yang, the perfect balance of energy."

Junco Sato Pollack. *Rimpa Gold and Silver*, 1995, revised in 2017.
Diptych: 120″ × 60″ (each)
Materials: first layer: woven silver / silk organza fabric with dye sublimation
applied by heat-compression printing, embellished with applied gold and silver
leaf; second layer: woven aluminum / polyester organza fabric with holography
applied on the aluminum coating
Techniques: applying gold and silver leaf, dye-sublimating, heat-transfer printing, hand-creasing, heat-compressing, stitching, heat-fusing holographic etching
Photo courtesy of the artist

Junco Sato Pollack. *Kinhin Series #1: Auspicious Beginning* 観自在, 2013. 28″ × 36″.
Materials: metallic threads and disperse dyes on pleated polyester organza and polyester taffeta
Techniques: stitching, heat-compressing, heat-transfer printing
Photo courtesy of the artist

*This incident inspired me to depict ocean waves, the heron's flight, my footsteps on the beach, the sunset, a sense of calm, and how nature heals and inspires. All my work expresses an awakening moment, or realization.*

"Between 2006 and 2019, I grieved the loss of many significant others, including my father and my guru of Kriya Yoga. When faced with so much deep loss, I found my work reverting to stitching, making *kesa*, which are monk's robes and mandalas—forms of Buddhist art made for an offering at temple or as meditation aids.

"Also during this time, I turned sixty years old. In the Eastern astrological calendar, this milestone is known as Kanreki, in which your zodiac calendar returns to the beginning point of a sixty-year cycle. I am living the cycle for the second time, therefore, and hopefully ascending the spiral of space and time with wisdom.

"The Kinhin series (walking meditation) comprises seven works that I executed during the years I was immersed in my healing meditation and simultaneously working in my studio, using stitching as my healing practice. Art making, meditation on the work, and stitching become an act of art, realization, and healing."

*Action with time is the key in healing pain that clings to your heart. I found that stitching was the right medium for this period in my life.*

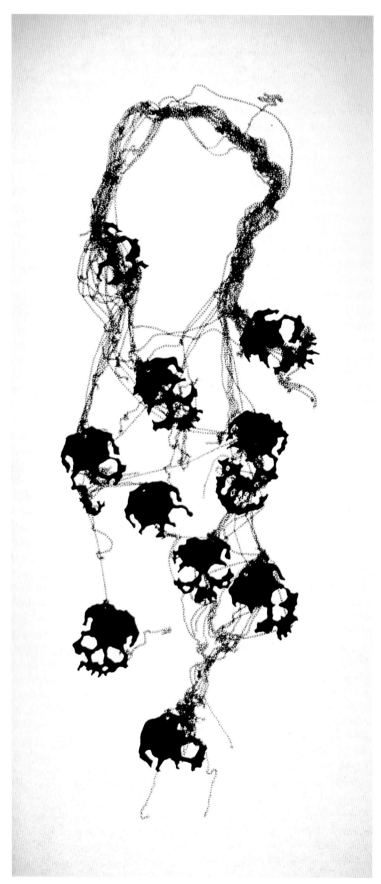

Urmas Lüüs. *Mortal Kombat: LOVE*,
2016. Variable size.
Materials: recycled bicycle, oxidized
brass chain
Techniques: cold-treating, oxidizing
Photo courtesy of the artist

# 40. Urmas Lüüs

WWW.URMASLUUS.COM
HAAPSALU, ESTONIA

In 2015, the artist was hit by a car while he was bicycling.

"It almost killed me. Months later, I was still having flashbacks and a feeling that my heart wasn't beating. I wasn't sure if I was still alive.

"Later, I got my broken bike back from the police department and I decided to use it in my art. For *Mortal Kombat: LOVE*, I wanted to represent the strong feelings that had overwhelmed me. I started to cut out skulls from the frame and then I connected them with a net of chains.

"The process of making the skulls and chains became a form of psychotherapy in that I analyzed what had happened to me and how to move forward from it. When I eventually went to a psychiatrist, she said I'd already done most of my therapy on my own."

*I made this piece for myself, but we are all similar in that we all have strong feelings, problems, and pain at times. I love to translate these feelings into a visual language. It gives me relief because it gets my thoughts out of my head, and perhaps it gives others solace to know they are not alone with their strong feelings. After finishing* Mortal Kombat: LOVE, *I felt serenity, very calm. I felt I confronted my fears and took time to understand my feelings.*

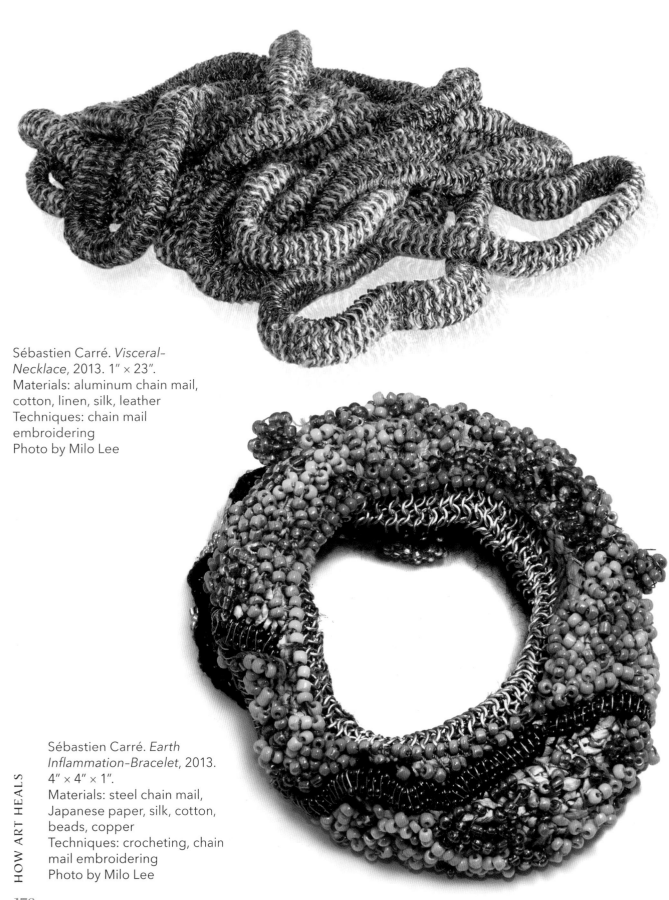

Sébastien Carré. *Visceral-Necklace*, 2013. 1″ × 23″.
Materials: aluminum chain mail, cotton, linen, silk, leather
Techniques: chain mail embroidering
Photo by Milo Lee

Sébastien Carré. *Earth Inflammation-Bracelet*, 2013. 4″ × 4″ × 1″.
Materials: steel chain mail, Japanese paper, silk, cotton, beads, copper
Techniques: crocheting, chain mail embroidering
Photo by Milo Lee

# 41. Sébastien Carré

WWW.SEBASTIENCARRE.COM

STRASBOURG, FRANCE

"I had to change the way I made my pieces while I was still in art school in Strasbourg because I was diagnosed with Crohn's disease (inflammation of the intestines). I lost a huge amount of weight and lost my strength as a result. I found it easier to work with textile techniques.

"It took six months of treatment before my pain died down. During that period, aluminum thread was the only kind of metal I was able to use. I started to produce work that represented human intestines. *Visceral–Necklace* was the first.

"Creating this piece felt like a kind of gestation. I worked on it all day for many months. It was an interactive piece; it had its own character as it lay alongside me on my bed, where I had to work because of my lack of strength."

*The process of manufacturing* Visceral–Necklace *helped me cope with my pain. The repeated movements put me into a kind of trance. Also, it was kind of a catharsis and an ex-voto. Even if I couldn't cure my body, I found an allegoric solution. It is the most personal piece I've created.*

Sébastien produced *Earth Inflammation–Bracelet* while in the hospital.

"I had tests every day for three days and wasn't allowed to eat. Instead of getting crazy about being hungry, I decided to focus on making a new art piece. It was the first I created using green, and I really do think it was my way of fighting back against the white sterility of the hospital. It reminded me of the outdoors, the land, even if I wasn't able to be out in nature."

Joan Hall. *Gatekeeper*, 2012. 17" × 7" × 3".
Materials: wood, ivory, metal
Techniques: assemblage
Photo courtesy of the artist

# 42. Joan Hall
WWW.JOANHALLCOLLAGE.COM
NEW YORK, USA

After Joan recovered from a serious illness, she felt motivated to make *Gatekeeper*.

"I had a feeling of new beginnings. This piece represented a door opening to a new chapter of my life."

*While making this piece, I was inspired by the lovely ivory, smiling face. I felt satisfied when it was completed. It reflected my hopefulness.*

. . . . . . . . . . . . . . . . . . . . . . . . . . . . . . . . . . . . . . . . . . .

*By making art, we create a world where we can communicate when we are laughing or hurting, and our sentiments are not met with judgment, and we don't risk rejection. We can be exactly who we are.*

Arielle Brackett. *Defense Mechanism One*, 2014. 8″ × 13″ × 0.5″.
Materials: brass, copper, silver, maple, African porcupine quills
Techniques: fabricating, engraving, hammering, riveting, drilling, woodworking
Photo courtesy of the artist

# 43. Arielle Brackett
WWW.ARIELLEBRACKETT.COM
OREGON, USA

"While creating *Defense Mechanism One*, I realized I very often became guarded and defensive when dealing with conflict with loved ones. I thought a lot about how I could visually represent self-protection and aggression. I thought about the ways that plants pour energy into themselves to grow. I, too, was putting a lot of energy into protecting myself."

*When I completed this piece, I felt a sense of relief. It was helpful to see a physical embodiment of the anger and defensiveness I had been feeling. I felt empowered in that I acknowledged this behavior, and that I understood where it had originated. The realization of how my destructive behaviors were hurting me allowed me to grow.*

Arielle was motivated to create the locket she calls *Family Agreements* while she processed her feelings about sexual abuse.

"I was still trying to understand my feelings of hurt, betrayal, and sadness surrounding my molestation. When I revealed my secret to my extended family, most of my relatives pretended it didn't happen, and maintained their relationships with my abusers. Only after I moved away from my hometown did I begin to heal. I was twenty-five when I moved; the physical distance enabled me to get strong and move on."

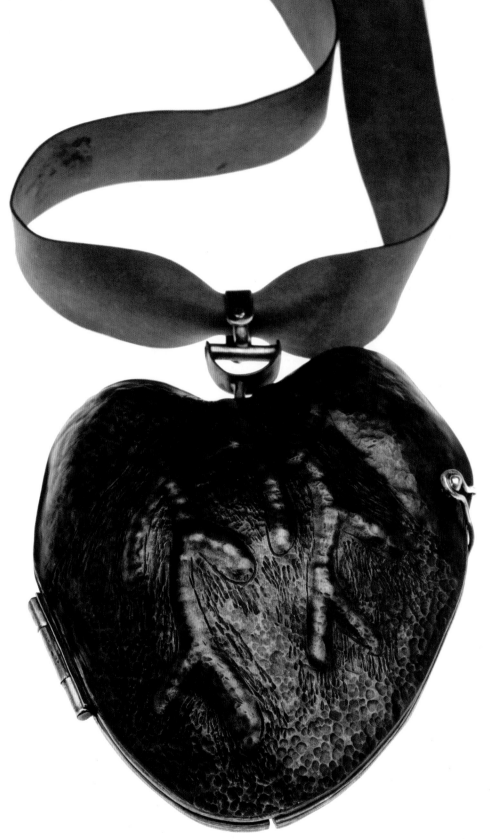

Arielle Brackett. *Family Agreements*,
2014. 6″ × 3.75″ × 1.35″.
Materials: copper, bronze, paper,
magnets, rubber
Techniques: centrifugal casting,
riveting, fabricating, chasing,
repoussage
Photo courtesy of the artist

*After making this piece, I presented it to a classroom of my peers. I was very nervous but got through it. I cried on my way home and then felt extremely proud of myself because I did a hard thing by revealing my abuse. I felt strong. It transformed my life. To this day, it's the hardest piece I've ever made.*

Arielle Brackett. *Family Agreements* (detail).
Photo courtesy of the artist

Linda Stephen. *Our Band*, 2010. 38″ × 46″ × 2″.
Materials: Japanese handcrafted papers, including *yuzen* hand-silk-screened fabric papers, *unryu* mulberry papers, *momogami* wrinkled papers, and marbled papers; PVA acid-free bookbinding adhesive
Technique: invented origami (folded paper), collaging
Photo by Terri I. Huss

# 44. Linda Stephen
WWW.LINDASTEPHEN.COM
NEBRASKA, USA

Linda began creating folded paper, or origami art, in 2003, using brightly colored, handcrafted Japanese papers.

"Inspired by the Minden Opera House and the community of Minden, Nebraska, *Our Band* is meant to celebrate the community and talent of small towns as well as the gifts they share with each new generation.

"At a time when small towns are dying, the Minden town square, surrounding a courthouse and park, is full of shops and restaurants. People greet one another, trucks stop for pedestrians, and volunteers put together a community theater production.

"My mother had just entered a nursing home when I created *Our Band*. She was suffering from a devastating degenerative brain disease that had slowly robbed her of speech and balance. I had been mourning her progressive losses for six years. It was a very sad time for me personally.

"On the other hand, it was a good time for me professionally. I was working with governments to design new urban towns and mixed-use walkable places. I was feeling proud, worthwhile, energetic, and optimistic."

*When I completed* Our Band, *I felt relief that the long work was done. I also felt pride and satisfaction. Because it includes three-dimensional sculptures, there are always shadows that make the piece feel alive. They change with the light in the room and the time of day. The images have the feel of downtown and remind me of the pride the parents there have in hearing their children making music.*

Linda's work *The Path through the Corn Maze* represents a celebration of fall.

"I love the scent of falling leaves, the bright colors of maples, the yellow of birches and aspen, picking and eating apples from the orchard, the golden afternoon light of the sun. I've been to a corn maze every autumn with my children. Creating this piece was a way to capture a joyful day in the season.

"For me, origami is a metaphor for the potential that lies within each person, each neighborhood, each city, and each country. One flat piece of paper, a simple material, through a multifaceted progression of folds, can be transformed into almost any image."

*When I completed* The Path through the Corn Maze, *I felt joy and pride. I loved how the hand-dyed Japanese papers looked like cornstalks and husks, and the feeling of depth of the children walking into the path. I was also relieved that the piece was finished. It is a slow process of many steps: choosing papers, folding hundreds of sculptures, laying out and carefully gluing down layer upon layer of origami sculptures. It was sort of like building a house from the foundation up.*

Linda Stephen. *The Path through the Corn Maze*, 2013.
25″ × 16″ × 2″.
Materials: hundreds of invented origami sculptures plus layered papers including Nepalese Lokta paper, Japanese handmade papers, including *chigiri-e* hand-dyed papers, *yuzen chiyogami* hand-silk-screened papers, *momogami* wrinkled papers, and *unryu* mulberry papers; PVA acid-free bookbinding adhesive
Technique: invented origami (folded paper) and collage
Photo by Terri I. Huss

187

Silvia Levenson. *Christmas with Yours*, 1995. 6.5′ × 8′ × 9.8′.
Materials: mixed-media installation with glass, furniture, TV, found objects, video
Techniques: kiln-casting glass
Photo by Cristiano Vasalli, private collection

# 45. Silvia Levenson

WWW.SILVIALEVENSON.COM

LESA, ITALY

"I explore daily interpersonal interactions through installations and objects that show openly what is often felt but only whispered or kept secret. My work centers on this unspeakable space, which is often so small, located between what we can see and what we feel. I use glass to reveal those feelings.

"My piece *Christmas with Yours* exemplifies this idea of the presence of invisible and dangerous sentiments. In this small installation, I refer to family events during which strong emotions are being felt but are kept unspoken. These emotions are made visible with my use of the glass spikes floating above the family."

> *I use glass because I am fascinated by its ambiguity, the fact that it is both strong and fragile. We rely on it to protect us in our homes, for example, but it can break into pieces and hurt us. It becomes the ideal material to show the two facets of people as they interact with other. If they keep their unhappy or aggressive feelings at bay, they remain strong and safe, but also ultimately unknown. It is this paradox I want to address in my work.*

"*Until Death Do Us Part* depicts in glass a perfect wedding cake with an unexploded pink hand grenade on top.

"The grenade is a symbol of potential future tensions. The family is often equated with sanctuary—a place where individuals find love, safety, security, and shelter—but evidence shows it can also be a place that imperils lives. In some, drastic forms of violence are perpetuated against girls and women.

One-third of murdered women in the world are killed by a husband or partner.

"My creativity remains a mystery to me. I start to create my work from an image or a feeling, and I cannot stop. Sometimes I am glad about the results, sometimes not. I wait for a while after I complete a piece. I need time to understand if I love or don't love what I made."

Silvia examines childhood and posits it encompasses a time of mystery and magic.

"The world of children is far from the world of adults, because children are not yet aware of what is good and what is evil. Childhood is a time during which the edge between reality and dreams is very evanescent. For a series of works called Strange Little Girl, I created sculptures but also collages, using pictures from my own childhood combined with masks of animals. I mixed animal heads with children's bodies to emphasize the dreamlike and unreal world of children.

"Society likes to think of childhood as a happy and carefree period. You see in advertisements pictures of smiling, laughing children. Children are expected to act this way, and they do their best to live up to these expectations and therefore please the adults around them. For example, they must smile so as not to ruin the family photo album.

"But I refuse to think of childhood as 'the carefree years,' to be looked back on with nostalgia. The children in my work are uncertain. They do not know where they are going and what is to happen."

Silvia Levenson. *Familia*, 2015.
11" × 15".
Materials: ink, paper
Techniques: glass printing
Photo courtesy of the artist

Silvia Levenson. *Until Death Do Us Part*, 2009.
20" × 15" × 15".
Materials: glass
Techniques: kiln-casting glass
Photo by Marco Del Comune, courtesy Bullseye
Projects, Portland OR

*For Familia, I used an old photo of my family.
Originally, it showed my maternal grandfather, his
brothers, and my great grandfather. I don't know a
lot about them, other than they lived in a rural
area where life is very hard and isolated. It is also
a place where women and children are not
respected or treated well. I don't know if my great-
grandfather was such a wolf, but I tried, with this
piece, to clean up my genealogical tree.*

Amy Tavern. *Forget Me Not*, 2014. 21.25″ × 3.75″ × 25″.
Materials: sterling silver, spray paint, photo, hair, acrylic
Techniques: fabricating, painting, scratching
Photo by Hank Drew

# 46. Amy Tavern
WWW.AMYTAVERN.COM
CALIFORNIA, USA

"When my father was diagnosed with Alzheimer's disease, I moved home to help take care of him. Because Alzheimer's can be a slow progression, I started grieving before his actual death. *Forget Me Not* reflects this time.

"When I began, I tried to make a piece about happy memories and feelings, but I could not. My mind was focused on the present, and I dwelled in sadness over the thought of losing him. This piece is based on the style and imagery of Victorian mourning jewelry. *Forget Me Not* is a silhouette of a classic, faceted jet necklace with a locket. Inside is a photograph of my father and a lock of his hair."

*To complete this piece, I went into a deep meditative state that allowed me to focus my attention and let feelings come to the surface, charging the work with my emotion. I can't remember exactly how I felt when it was completed, but probably a mixture of relief, reverence, sadness, longing, and satisfaction.*

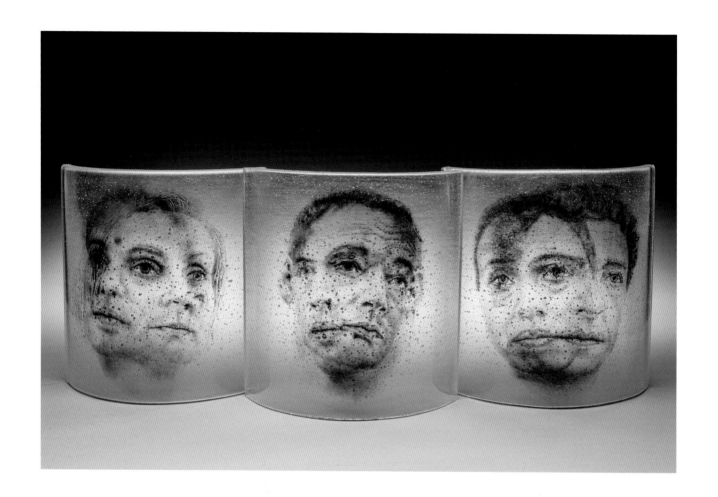

Michael Janis. *Echoes*, 2015. 9.5" × 9.5" × 5" (each).
Materials: glass, glass powder imagery
Techniques: fusing glass with sgraffito
Photo by Pete Duvall

# 47. Michael Janis
WWW.MICHAELJANIS.COM
WASHINGTON, DC, USA

"The Society for Contemporary Craft, in Pittsburgh, Pennsylvania, was planning a traveling exhibition titled 'Mindful: Exploring Mental Health through Art,' intended to understand mental health through the lens of contemporary craft. I wanted to express my experience with my family's mental health issues, and our struggles with understanding and dealing with these issues.

"For *Echoes*, I wanted to explore how we live so often in a condition of being obscured from ourselves and others. I see the interaction of the nonaligned faces in the glass artwork as a depiction of both our inner and outer worlds. I wanted to show a sense of connection between those worlds. Using clear glass as the main medium was a way of 'seeing through' one's actions and intents. To me, the medium and the message worked together."

*I felt invigorated as I created this artwork, with each aspect of it often encouraging exploration of other facets, and I had to keep focused on telling the strongest and most concise story for the artwork.*

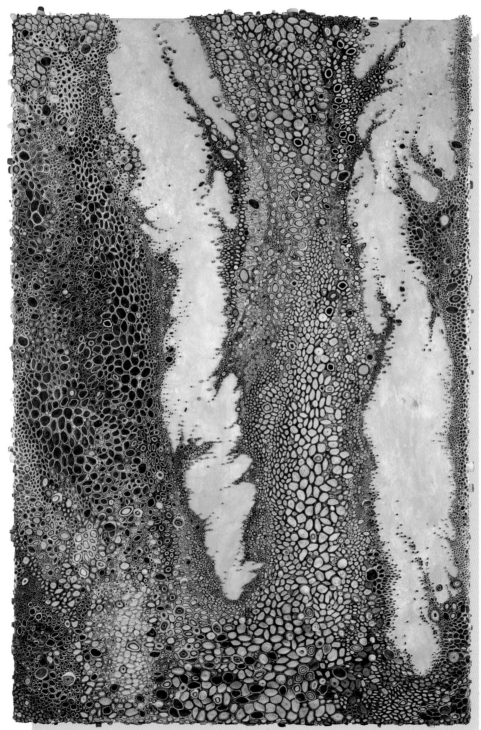

Amy Genser.
*Neptune*, 2018.
60″ × 90″ × 5″.
Materials: paper
and acrylic on
canvas
Technique: rolling,
cutting, gluing
paper
Photo by Paul
Lowicki

# 48. Amy Genser
WWW.AMYGENSER.COM
CONNECTICUT, USA

"For *Neptune*, I was inspired by the aerial view of the Connecticut shore-line. I am in awe of the lines and shapes created where water meets land. I was imagining the coast in the summer, when colors are crisp, clear, vibrant, and bright. It's a joyful expression."

*I was happy with the finished piece. Working on a piece this size is a commitment, because it's in production for a few months. It claimed a lot of real estate in my studio. But I love being invested in a piece for a period of time. It motivates me to get into the studio to keep going, and I feel very alive in the process. It's like I'm helping a tree grow and having to fertilize it every step of the way. I feel like this is one of my strongest pieces.*

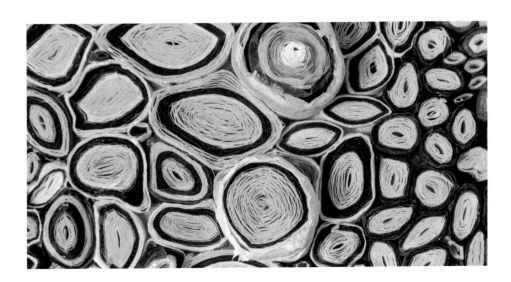

Barb Olson. *Tea Bag Dress*, 2015.
57" × 35".
Materials: used tea bags, thread,
ink, paint, cotton/silk voile
Techniques: stitching tea bags
together, printing, writing,
painting, layering, hand-quilting
Photo by Ken Sanville

# 49. Barb Olson
WWW.BARBOLSON.NE
COLORADO, USA

"This piece, *Tea Bag Dress* in the Dress series, was done throughout many stages of processing and healing from my divorce after a forty-year marriage. The feelings I expressed in the series ranged from anger, rage, hurt, betrayal, and loss to hope, delight, self-confidence, and insight."

*I process emotions by quiet reflection. Working with tea bags, stitching them together, then printing on them spoke to this process. At the same time, it was also fun exploring my curiosity about using this paper medium. It was delightful to see how successful it turned out. I felt really accomplished at trying something new and creating it each step of the way. It was very satisfying.*

Rea Rossi. *Resound*, 2015. 12″ × 13″ × 4.8″.
Materials: three-dimensional printed nylon
Techniques: three-dimensional printing
Photo courtesy of the artist

# 50. Rea Rossi
WWW.REA-STUDIOART.COM
NEW JERSEY, USA

"I was born with a genetic bilateral sensorineural hearing loss and rely on hearing aids to amplify and clarify sounds that are otherwise subdued or incomprehensible. My work explores my experience with deafness.

"I use a computer-aided three-dimensional modeling program called Rhinoceros. Within a virtual program, I design unique forms. I take a single form and multiply it ad infinitum. I flow the pieces along a curve that twists and turns, allowing them to entwine and interlace with each other, producing a complex network.

"To me, this construction of overlapping parts relates to the sensation of processing language and sounds as a deaf person. When I am in a room with many people, and everyone is talking over one other, with added background noise, I feel overwhelmed. I compensate for my inability to understand everything by focusing on visual movements of the mouth and facial expressions. It is common for me to need repetition and clarification.

"There is a common misconception that when a deaf person wears hearing aids or has had 'corrective' surgery, such as a cochlear implant, that they are 'cured,' that they are no longer deaf. This notion puts a huge burden on people with hearing loss to work harder to conform to the mainstream 'hearing' world.

"My hope is that my artwork will challenge some of the widespread misconceptions about the deaf community and promote reform regarding how disabilities are perceived. To me, an inability to do something means there is a challenge. Solutions are possible. There are so many ways to make the world a more accessible place for anyone who may need accommodations.

"I created the neckpiece *Resound* from a single form that closely resembles one of the three tiny bones, the malleus, in the inner ear canal. All three of these tiny bones fit on a dime. They pick up on the vibrations of sound waves that pass through the ear drum and play an integral part in our ability to hear.

"The title of *Resound* was derived from a brand of hearing aids that I've worn for many years. This piece is a statement piece—one can put it on and feel regal and appear so to viewers. It is bold and fashionable, contrary to the design aesthetic of modern-day hearing aids, which is meant to be discreet and invisible. Not only is there a stigma against wearing hearing aids, but also there is the financial burden of purchasing them, because insurance companies consider them to be a luxury item."

> *My body of work was created in the hope of opening the conversation and awareness of deafness, and to help facilitate developments in design approaches for hearing devices. Just as glasses have become personal and fashionable, I want hearing aids to be so as well.*

"I grew up in the hearing (mainstream) world. I learned American Sign Language when I went to college at Rochester Institute of Technology (RIT), where there is the National Technical Institute for the Deaf (NTID). Prior to attending RIT/NTID, I did not know many people outside my family who had hearing loss. I knew very little to nothing about deaf culture or deaf history.

"Attending college there was a huge turning point in my life. I became immersed in an incredibly rich and diverse community of deaf people, with an incredible amount of pride and abilities. I felt, for the first time, a sense of purpose as a deaf individual and even more so as an artist."

Rea Rossi. *Resonance,* 2013. 8″ × 6.5″ × 4″. Materials: nylon Techniques: three-dimensional printing Photo courtesy of the artist

Resonance, *a three-dimensional printed nylon bangle, takes on the shape of the outer ear. Its structure is a beautiful and complex balance between dense and delicate parts throughout the piece.*

# Additional Artists

These artists are featured in the exclusive web portion of this book. You can find their art and stories here: www.schifferbooks.com/HowArtHeals

1. Rob Kolhouse
*www.kolhouse.com*
*Arizona, USA*

2. Margie LaLonde
*www.instagram.com/margie*
*.lalonde*
*New York, USA*

3. Shivani Aggarwal
*www.shivaniaggarwal.art*
*Delhi, India*

4. Marian Zielinski
*www.marianzielinski.com*
*Georgia, USA*

5. Kerri Blackman
*www.dailypaintworks.com*
*/artists/kerri-blackman-5119*
*/artwork*
*Oregon, USA*

6. Ellen Fuller
*www.ellenfuller.com*
*New Mexico, USA*

7. Stiofan O'Ceallaigh
*www.stiofanoceallaigh.co.uk*
*West Yorkshire, UK*

8. Aryana B. Londir
*www.aryanalondir.com*
*Arizona, USA*

9. Judy Coates Perez
*www.judycoatesperez.com*
*California, USA*

10. Margaret Blank
*www.margaretblank.com*
*Alberta, Canada*

11. Colleen Ansbaugh
*www.ColleenAnsbaugh.com*
*Wisconsin, USA*

12. Karen S. Musgrave
*www.musgrave.karen*
*@gmail.com*
*Illinois, USA*

13. Melody Money
*www.melodymoney.com*
*Colorado, USA*

14. Kim Svoboda
*www.kimsvoboda@mac.com*
*New, York USA*

15. Geneviève Attinger
*www.attinger-art-textile*
*.odexpo.com*
*Pontivy, France*

16. Sue Lewis
*www.sustudioblog@*
*wordpress.com*
*Colorado, USA*

17. Lynne Brotman
*www.lynnebrotmanfiberart*
*.com*
*Texas, USA*

18. Merill Comeau
*www.merillcomeau.com*
*Massachusetts, USA*

19. Patricia Hardie
*www.pathardie.com*
*Merrickville, Canada*

20. Demry Frankenheimer
*www.DemryArt.com*
*Colorado, USA*

21. Janice Stevens
*www.Janicestevensquilts.com*
*Suratthani, Thailand*

22. Gwyned Trefethen
*www.gwnedtrefethen.com*
*Massachusetts, USA*

23. Lin Bentley Keeling
*www.LinBentleyKeeling.com*
*Texas, USA*

24. Harriet Cherry Cheney
*www.harrietcheney.com*
*New York, USA*

25. Grace Gee
*www.Gracegeeart.com*
*Colorado, USA*

26. Isabelle Wiessler
*www.isabelle-wiessler.de*
*Gundelfingen, Germany*

27. Mary Louise Gerek
*www.mlfiberarts.com*
*Colorado, USA*

28. Norma Minkowitz
*www.normaminkowitz.com*
*Connecticut, USA*

29. Fei Su
*https://feisu.weebly.com*
*Edmonton, Canada*

30. Rose Clancy
*www.roseclancy.com*
*Pennsylvania, USA*

31. Kathryn Rousso
*www.kathy_rousso@*
*hotmail.com*
*Alaska, USA*

32. Sharon Peoples
*www.sharon-peoples.com*
*Australian Capital Territory,*
*Australia*

33. Kazuki Takizawa
*www.kazukitakizawa.com*
*California, USA*

34. Shona Wilson
*www.shonawilson.com*
*New South Wales, Australia*

35. Terri Grant
*www.terrigrantart.com*
*Benton City, WA*

36. Don Sexton
*www.sextonart.com*
*New York, USA*

37. Deborah L. Brand
*www.DeborahLBrand.com*
*New York, USA*

38. Deidre Scherer
*www.Dscherer.com*
*Vermont, USA*

39. John Moran
*www.backdoorart.com*
*Temse, Belgium*

40. Cynthia Lee
*www.cynthiajlee.com*
*Illinois, USA*

41. Ellie Reinhold
*www.elliereinhold.com*
*North Carolina, USA*

42. Mary-Ellen Latino
*www.highinfiberart.com*
*Massachusetts, USA*

43. Melanie Vote
*www.melanievote.com*
*New York, USA*

44. Angela Treat Lyon
*www.AngelaTreatLyonART*
*.com*
*California, USA*

# An Invitation to All

If you would like to share your collages, I've created a dedicated Facebook page for just that purpose. My hope is that everyone shares their experience with this technique, either by simply posting a photo of your work, or a photo and explanation of what the imagery represents to you. In doing so, we can offer one another a place of support and connection, and an opportunity to feel a sense of belonging while boosting our pleasure hormones.

PLEASE GO TO
https://www.facebook.com/groups/3119171991429353
(ART HEALS: Express your Feelings with Collage and Mixed Media) to participate.

# Bibliography

Bayles, David, and Ted Orland. *Art and Fear.* Santa Cruz, CA: Image Continuum, 1993.

Berman, Morris. *The Twilight of American Culture.* New York: W. W. Norton, 2000.

Cacciatore, Joanne. *Bearing the Unbearable: Love, Loss and the Heartbreaking Path of Grief.* Somerville, MA: Wisdom Publications, 2017.

David, Bertrand, and Jean-Jacques Lefrére. *The Oldest Enigma of Humanity: The Key to the Mystery of the Paleolithic Cave Paintings.* New York: Arcade, 2013.

Dissanayake, Ellen. *What Is Art For?* Seattle: University of Washington Press, 1988.

Ganim, Barbara. *Art and Healing: Using Expressive Art to Heal Your Body, Mind, and Spirit.* Novato, CA: Echo Point Books & Media, 2013.

Hickman, Richard. *Why We Make Art and Why It Is Taught.* Portland, OR: Intellect, 2005.

Kaimal, Giriia, Kendra Ray, and Juan Muniz. "Reduction of Cortisol Levels and Participants' Responses following Art Making." *Art Therapy: Journal of the American Art Therapy Association* 33, no. 2 (2016): 74–80.

King, Juliet L., ed. *Art Therapy, Trauma, and Neuroscience: Theoretical and Practical Perspectives.* Abingdon, UK: Routledge, 2016.

Lienhard, Dina A. "Roger Sperry's Split Brain Experiments (1959–1968)." In *Embryo Project Encyclopedia.* Tempe: Arizona State University, 2017. http://embryo.asu.edu /handle/10776/13034.

Liu, Yun-Zi, Yun-Xia Wang, and Chun-Lei Jiang. "Inflammation: The Common Pathway of Stress-Related Diseases." *Frontiers in Human Neuroscience* 11 (June 2017): 316. https://doi.org/10.3389 /fnhum.2017.00316.

Masciotra, David. "How America's 'Culture of Hustling' Is Dark and Empty." *The Atlantic,* August 13, 2013.

McNiff, Shaun. *Art as Medicine: Creating a Therapy of the Imagination.* Boulder, CO: Shambhala, 1992.

Rogers, Earl. *The Art of Grief: The Use of Expressive Arts in a Grief Support Group.* New York: Routledge, 2007.

Stellar, Jennifer E., Neha John-Henderson, Craig L. Anderson, Amie M. Gordon, Galen D. McNeil, and Dacher Keltner. "Positive Affect and Markers of Inflammation: Discrete Positive Emotions Predict Lower Levels of Inflammatory Cytokines." *Emotion* 15, no. 2 (2015): 129–33.

Stuckey, Heather L., and Jeremy Nobel. "The Connection between Art, Healing, and Public Health: A Review of Current Literature." *American Journal of Public Health* 10, no. 2 (2010): 254–63.

Thompson, Barbara E., and Robert A. Neimeyer, eds. *Grief and the Expressive Arts: Practices for Creating Meaning.* Abingdon, UK: Routledge, 2014.

# Resources

## ART THERAPY, HYPNOTHERAPY, AND PSYCHOTHERAPY RESOURCES

American Art Therapy Association, https://arttherapy.org

National Association of Social Workers, www.socialworkers.org

National Board for Certified Clinical Hypnotherapists, www.natboard.com

## COLLAGE ARTIST BLOGS AND TUTORIALS

Jane Davies, http://janedaviesstudios.com

Collage Artists of America, www.facebook.com/groups /collageartistsofamerica

France Papillon, www.france-papillon.com/ (especially the Journal on Monday videos)

Robert Burridge, www.youtube.com/watch?v=Ih7PfwLNfoU

John Evans, www.johnevansartstudio.com

Laura Lein-Svencner, www.lauralein-svencner.com

## COLLAGE WEBSITES

www.collageart.org

www.collagegallery.com/index.html

www.globalcollage.com

www.kolajmagazine.com

## BOOKS ON COLLAGE

Brommer, Gerald. *Collage Techniques: A Guide for Artists and Illustrators*. New York: Watson-Guptill, 1994.

Evans Stout, Roxanne. *Storytelling with Collage: Techniques for Layering, Color and Texture*. Oakland, CA: North Light Books, 2016.

Lein-Svencner, Laura. *Learn the Basics of Design with Collage: Instructional Guide*. San Francisco: Blurb, 2018.

McKechnie, Christine. *Paper Collage: Painted Paper Pictures*. Trent, UK: Search Press, 1995.

Plowman, Randel. *The Collage Workbook: How to Get Started and Stay Inspired*. New York: Lark Crafts, 2012.

St. Hilaire, Elizabeth. *Painted Paper Art Workshop: Easy and Colorful Collage Paintings*. Oakland, CA: North Light Books, 2016.

Talbot, Jonathan. *Collage: A New Approach; Collage without Liquid Adhesives*. 5th ed. Unionville, NY: Royal Fireworks, 2014.

## SUPPLIES FOR COLLAGE

Dick Blick, www.dickblick.com

Dharma Trading Company, www.dharmatrading.com

Michaels, www.michaels.com

Vycombe Arts UK, www.vycombe-arts.co.uk

## Work by Other Artists

If you want to read more artist stories—other than those presented in this book—and see their work, head over to **www.schifferbooks.com/HowArtHeals**.